ONCE-A-MONTH COOKING

ONCE-A-MONTH COOKING

A time-saving, budget-stretching plan to prepare delicious meals

Mimi Wilson and Mary Beth Lagerborg

PUBLISHING

Colorado Springs, Colorado

Copyright © 1986, 1992 by Mimi Wilson and Mary Beth Lagerborg
Published 1986 by St. Martin's Press. Second edition 1992 published by Focus on the Family Publishing.
This book was originally published in 1982 under the title *Freeze and Save* and in 1984 as *Dinner's Ready*.

Library of Congress Cataloging-in-Publication Data

Wilson, Mimi
    Once-a-Month cooking: a time-saving, budget-stretching plan to prepare delicious meals / Mimi Wilson and Mary Beth Lagerborg. — 2nd ed.
      p. cm.
    Includes index.
    ISBN 1-56179-041-9
    1. Make-ahead cookery.   I. Lagerborg, Mary Beth.   II. Title.
TX652/W566   1991
641.5'55—dc 20   91-46953
                                               CIP
Published by Focus on the Family Publishing, Colorado Springs, Colorado 80995.

Distributed in the U.S.A. and Canada by Word Books, Dallas, Texas.

Scripture quotations are from:
The Holy Bible, New International Version (NIV), copyright (c) 1973, 1978, 1984 by the International Bible Society.
The Living Bible (TLB), copyright (c) 1971 by Tyndale House Publishers.

Editor: Sheila Cragg
Designer and Illustrator: Bob Fuller

Printed in the United States of America

94 95 96 97 98 99 / 16 15 14 13 12 11

CONTENTS

ACKNOWLEDGMENTS

We are grateful to the following people who have provided professional advice, recipes, child care and encouragement—very important ingredients.

Our families:
Calvin, Kurt, Kindra and
  Kevin Wilson
Alex, Tim, Daniel and
  Andrew Lagerborg

Our neighbors, associates, relatives and friends:
Karen Abbotts
Pat Agnew
Jan and Tim Altman
Barbara Anderson
Deborah Ayres
Cynthia Bahlman
Jerilynn Blum
Diane Bogart
Paula Brown
Jim Burghardt
Elisabeth Chubb
Charlotte Cone
Dori Cooper
Connie Cox
Sheila Cragg

Robin Currier
Marlys DeVries
Chris Douglas
Irene L. Evans
Dolores Eyler
Jacci Folk
Ken and Diane Glass
Peg Goddard
Melita Hayes
Dona Henry
Roland Hieb
Liz Hurst
Susan Keaney
Laura Kuiken
Marjorie Kurz
Christine and Vincent
  Lagerborg
Debbie and David Lagerborg
Lorie Mae Leavitt
Carol Mathews
Judy McBride
Bonnie McCullough
Anne Metzler

Judy Miller
Georgiana Morrill
Mardell Peterson
Kathy Pitzer
Dave Plummer
Norene Rask
Karen Seeling
Virginia Shane
Bill and Ella Spees
Clarinda Spees
Sue Stockman
Paul and Linda Stowell
Dotty Thur
Kathy Voss
Barbara West
Carol West
Dawn Wilson
Deborah Wilson
Don and Chris Wilson
Kent and Debbie Wilson
Tricia Woodyard

INTRODUCTION

"Sirs," he said, "please don't go any further. Stop awhile and rest here in the shade of this tree while I get water to refresh your feet, and a bite to eat to strengthen you. Do stay awhile before continuing your journey."

(Abraham, Genesis 18:3-5, TLB).

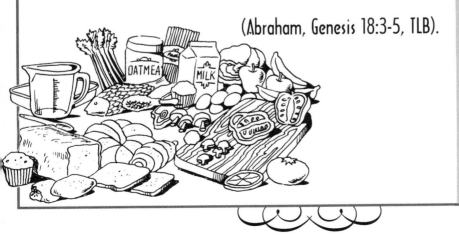

A warm welcome is easier when food is always on hand. Our method of cooking a month's dinners in a day and freezing them evolved from a desire to be ready to entertain at a moment's notice. My husband, Cal, and I decided early in our marriage that when company came, it wouldn't do for me to be swinging from the chandelier or wanting to string the children from it to keep them out of the way.

Once-a-Month Cooking is designed to help you achieve a welcoming environment and have stew always in the pot without being in there yourself. It's meant to be a practical help for busy women of all vocations, interests and needs.

I developed this plan, because I felt I had to do something drastic to squeeze more time into my day. I had three young children, a busy husband and company two or three times a week; plus I wanted to become involved with refugees. I used time studies to determine where I wasted the most time, and I found it was in making meals from scratch each day. It's not as if I went to the garden every day or killed the chickens for dinner. Even so, I believed I could save significant time in the kitchen.

I also wanted to reduce food waste. Our family had seen starvation firsthand during a visit to Africa and in working with refugees. We couldn't box up a meal and send it to an African child, but we could choose not to buy food and then throw it away. The money saved on food costs could be spent in so many better ways.

I began by cooking a week's dinners, then two and three weeks and finally a month of meals in one day. I found that the plan saved time in the kitchen and grocery store, and it minimized food waste. Since the method depended on careful planning, it resulted in a greater variety of meals and could be adapted to many family favorites.

In addition to all this, I desired to have a ministry of spontaneous hospitality. I grew up watching my mother, a missionary in Zaire, Africa, put together meals for anyone who traveled by our remote outpost. Visits were often unexpected. Even though we had to travel great distances to buy our food, Mother somehow prepared large meals and served our guests graciously.

She also taught me one of the most vivid lessons about the value of giving, not only meals but other possessions. One time a missionary family passed by our outpost in a rickety old car. The trunk lid was off, and the children were stuffed inside the trunk.

It was late afternoon, and when the sun sank below the forest trees, absolutely no one traveled, because it was extremely dark and unsafe. Mother invited the family to stay the night. She told me the family was as poor as church mice. I didn't know what that meant, but I knew the family needed our help.

The next day, when they were about to leave, I went to my toy box and pulled out my broken doll, the puzzles with the pieces missing and the wind-up toys that didn't work. The children were thrilled to receive my toys since they didn't have anything.

As I watched them happily climb into the car's trunk, I turned to Mother, fully expecting her to tell me how gracious I had been to share my toys.

"Weren't they happy with our things?" I said.

"You're the only one who knows if you've given your very best," Mother replied.

Mother didn't make that remark as a rebuke; it was more a longing that I would know what it was like to give my very best. Watching the way she gave to those who passed by our outpost, I learned from her example. Mother exemplified Jesus' request that we feed and care for those in need.

While Jesus was attending a banquet, He said to the host, "When you give a luncheon or dinner, do not invite your friends, your brothers or relatives, or your rich neighbors; if you do, they may invite you back and so you will be repaid. But when you give a banquet, invite the poor, the crippled, the lame, the blind, and you will be blessed" (Luke 14:12-14a, NIV).

As a result of my mother's influence, I began a ministry of sharing food and offering hospitality. Cal and I are missionaries in Ecuador, where I cook by the once-a-month plan. This allows me more valuable time with my family and to work with handicapped individuals. I also teach my food preparation method to women.

Cal is a family physician. He trains Ecuadorian doctors and heads a team of dentists and doctors for a clinic on the northern coast of Ecuador for people without other medical help.

Often people will come to our home for counsel regarding physical or spiritual concerns. I frequently invite them to stay for a meal. I've found that once their physical needs are met, they are more open to share on a deeper level.

In addition, we have seen our children's lives enriched as people of all ages and from other countries gather around our table. Our children have learned to discern when people are hurting, to ask appropriate questions and to speak easily with and appreciate different types of people.

Moreover, it feels good to have meals on hand whether for our own families or for those with a special need. The woman of Proverbs planned ahead. The oil for her lamps did not run out, her family was clothed against the cold, and she probably kept her maidens busy preparing food akin to the once-a-month cooking method. Since she planned ahead, her time was freed for so many other concerns, like reaching out to the poor and needy.

Mimi Wilson

As a longtime friend of Mimi Wilson's I can attest that this book represents only a morsel of her wisdom on hospitality. Her passion is to serve the Lord faithfully with her resources, her energies, her home and her family. She desires to meet the needs of others rather than being caught up by a comfortable, fashionable form of entertaining.

She has dedicated herself to the practice of hospitality for the last twenty years, through lean years and fatter ones, often to the point of exhaustion. But the blessings the Wilsons have received are significant: They've seen the Lord provide for their needs (including the need for rest) over and over again. They've had the privilege of introducing many to Jesus Christ. And they enjoy friendships with people from all over the world.

For several years, our family has been on the receiving end of the Wilsons' hospitality. I'll never forget the time we were vacationing in Colorado and asked Mimi to keep our infant son overnight, which she gladly did. Afterward I found out it had been her birthday, and she had taken Timmy with her to a family birthday dinner at a restaurant.

One of my favorite memories of a meal at Mimi's was a breakfast just days before the Wilsons moved to Ecuador. While our families were eating in the breakfast room, movers were carrying the dining room furniture out the front door.

My desire is to share Mimi's insights on hospitality so you can apply them in prac-

tical and personal ways. One reason this cooking method is ideal for company is that the main entrée has been prepared ahead, so having guests can be more spontaneous and fun.

If you aren't sure what to prepare or don't have time to fix a big meal, *Once-a-Month Cooking* offers a wide variety of entrées to choose from. You can even invite friends or family over at the last minute. If unexpected company arrives, you won't have to scramble to fix a meal or go out for food, because your main dish will be ready to cook and serve. If at least part of the meal is ready, more time is left to make a special salad or dessert, set a nice table, pick up the living room or soak in the tub before your company arrives.

Extending hospitality doesn't need to be fancy or expensive. When we entertain, we're often caught up by appearances, by how nice our home looks or by our cooking expertise (or lack thereof). As a result, we tend to shy away from having people over. If we concentrate less on impressing others with our ability to entertain, however, we can focus more on hospitality that builds bridges of concern, caring and availability.

Besides giving you more opportunities to open your home to others, this cooking plan can be used for a ministry of hospitality on the go. Using small, disposable dishes, you can freeze single or double portions of certain entrées for shut-ins. You can either take the dish with prepara-

tion instructions or cook it and take it ready to serve.

Delivering a delicious, homemade meal, flowers and a special baked goody is a way to comfort the lonely. If you have children, let them help you take food to an elderly friend. Your children's youthfulness is a special tuck-in gift.

Taking a hot dish to those who are sick, hurting or have had a death in the family is a meaningful way to offer comfort and care. One day Mimi received word that a dear friend, an older man, had died on the operating table. She had an entrée out of her freezer and a meal to the family's home before they returned from the hospital.

Preparing meals for people with long-term health or stress problems is also especially helpful, since those people are often forgotten as the months go by. My son Tim's first grade teacher had been away from the classroom for several weeks following major surgery. Alone and single, she was discouraged and missed her students. Another student's mother and I were able to put together a meal quickly. Our children delivered the meal to their teacher and ate with her by candlelight.

Giving a week or two of dinner dishes to a mom anticipating the arrival of a baby is not only a great gift to her, but also to her family. Mimi asks the mother-to-be to grocery shop with one of the month's lists from this book. The next day, Mimi goes to her friend's home, prepares a month of dinner entrées and puts

them away in the friend's own containers and freezer.

One woman wrote that she cooks meals this way for her elderly parents when she visits them in another state. She then has the peace of mind of knowing they're eating well.

Each of us knows people to whom a warm meal would be a great blessing: elderly relatives or neighbors, a single person, a friend who has been ill or a hurting family. Throughout the book, we've interspersed more tips on how to share your entrées with others.

Besides being ideal for a ministry of caring and hospitality, this method is also beneficial in a wide variety of situations. Busy career people, including nurses, doctors, midwives, flight attendants and accountants at tax time, have benefited from this plan. They have found that putting these meals together—perhaps with the help of their mate—relieves the nightly five o'clock pressure.

The plan is perfect for moms who carpool kids in the afternoon or work odd or late hours. It's an immense help for women before the arrival of a baby or if a family member is anticipating major surgery.

It's great for the mother who ordinarily cooks with a child on one hip and another hanging from her leg. Young children are usually fussy at dinnertime, and Mom is tired enough to be fussy herself. Home-schooling moms have also used this plan to teach their children about food prepa-

ration and cooking measurements.

Meals on hand save the day when a family is moving from one place to another or is remodeling the kitchen or any other part of the house. They're also great to take on vacation to a cabin, so Mom can get some rest from the usual chores.

Finally, if you don't feel like serving an entrée from the freezer, you can still prepare one of your favorites. The plan frees you to choose whether you want to cook, take food out or use a dish you already have on hand.

After you've prepared a month or two weeks of meals, you won't have to fall back on less-nutritious, quick-fix foods or the more costly eating out. If you have a hectic schedule, you won't have to figure out what on earth you can fix for dinner and still make it to an evening meeting on time.

We hope this method will prove as helpful to you as it has been to us. It's our prayer that the Lord will open ways you can uniquely serve Him with your time, your abilities and your possessions, and that you can make hospitality a family affair.

Mary Beth Lagerborg

CHAPTER  1

"Cheerfully share your home with those who need a meal or a place to stay for the night"

(1 Peter 4:9, TLB).

One Saturday at lunchtime, John and his friend Chris were shooting baskets. John's mother, Nancy, invited Chris to stay for lunch. After serving the boys grilled cheese sandwiches, apple slices, potato chips and a glass of milk, she returned to her work.

From the kitchen Nancy overheard Chris say, "Wow, does your mom fix lunches like that all the time? My mom doesn't do lunches, and for dinner we pick a frozen dinner out of the freezer."

Chris was from a loving family, but meals were not a high priority. Many mothers with busy schedules find that the time-consuming task of preparing meals has become overwhelming. They find that they're opting for fast foods, frozen din-

ners and eating out more often than they would like.

All of us with growing children want them to eat nutritious meals. We want the family to enjoy their time together around the dinner table as much as possible. And we would like our meals to magically appear on time each evening. *Once-a-Month Cooking* was born out of a desire to meet those needs.

The benefits of cooking this way are great for any family. You'll save money on the food budget while enjoying the satisfaction of knowing your family is eating well. You'll also save energy for the family cook and gain greater flexibility to meet needs outside the kitchen.

OVERVIEW OF THE PLAN

Before you get out the pots and pans and fix a batch of meals, here are a few hints to help you adapt once-a-month cooking to your lifestyle.

First, it's an easy system you can follow to prepare two weeks or one month of main-meal dishes at a time. Each entrée is partially prepared or cooked and assembled in advance, put into sealed containers and stored in the freezer. When you're ready to serve a certain meal, all you have to do is thaw it, combine the ingredients and cook the entrée. The advantage of this method is that you do all your

time-consuming preparation and cleanup at one time.

Second, as good as this plan sounds, you might protest, "I can't cook that way. I don't have a separate freezer."

You can store a month of meals in your refrigerator freezer by putting many of them in freezer bags instead of hard containers. At first you may not have room for ice cream, juices and bread, but as you use the entrées, you can begin adding those food items. (Whether your freezer is large or small, cleaning it out before cooking day will be a big help.)

Third, the recipes for this book were not tried in stainless steel test-kitchens but were tested over and over in numerous homes by women of various cooking abilities. Recipes were chosen for variety and good nutrition and call for regular rather than exotic ingredients. The meals are not gourmet fare but tasty dishes your family will enjoy and you will be pleased to serve to company.

Fourth, each dish makes between four and twelve servings. The average number of servings per entrée is about six. Depending on the ages of your children, if you have four members or fewer in your family, you may want to divide each entrée into two or more meal-size portions. Even larger families will often have leftovers for lunches or after-school snacks for hungry children. The meals come in handy for many occasions.

Furthermore, grocery-shopping guidelines and preparation techniques are offered in this chapter. The second chapter offers a two-week cycle of recipes. The shorter plan is useful for someone who wants to try the system for the first time. It also works well for a smaller family or one with younger children. By dividing each entrée into a couple of portions, you can easily extend the two-week cycle to a month or more of dinner meals.

You will also find that most recipes in the two-week entrée plan appear again in other cycles and that it is a shortened version of the one-month plans. All the program recipes are printed in the order in which they'll be prepared, making the system easier to follow.

The mainstay of this method is the two, one-month cycles of recipes found in chapters 3 and 4. Your family will enjoy a wider variety of dishes if you alternate between those two cycles.

Depending on the size of your family and their appetites, you may also find that a month of entrées lasts two months. Some women actually prefer cooking every two months. If their families are larger, they stretch the plan by eating out and filling in with lighter meals or easy foods like hamburgers.

Since we have had numerous requests for low-fat dishes, we have included a two-week cycle of entrées for those who need to watch their fat intake. We also consulted a professional dietician to make sure the recipes met the criteria for low-fat foods. We think you'll find those meals every bit as tasty as the others.

At the beginning of each entrée plan, a sample calendar is included as an overview of the recipes you'll cook for that month. You, of course, will actually decide which day will be your cooking day and when you'll serve any particular dish. A blank calendar has been included in chapter 7; you can reproduce it to write in when you want to serve each entrée or to create your own cooking plan. That

chapter also shows you how to adapt the system to your own recipes.

In chapter 6, you'll find a few of our favorite bread, breakfast, dessert, salad and vegetable recipes. And chapter 8 offers sections on equivalent measures and freezer storage tips.

FOOD PREPARATION GUIDELINES

The first time you try the once-a-month method, we suggest you use one of the plans from this book. That's a much easier way to start rather than attempting to adapt the plan to your own recipes. If preparing a month's worth of dinner entrées in a day seems overwhelming, try one of the two-week plans.

It also works best to shop one day and cook the next. Food preparation and cooking take a full day or more. Further, it's important to read over the instructions for the plan you've chosen to follow, since you'll need to prepare some food the day before you do the major cooking.

Some women have found that the long hours required to complete the one-month plan in a day were too exhausting. They recommend you shop one day; then spread the preparation and cooking over two more days. If you have a lot of stamina, you can shop one day and do all the cooking the next, but expect to have two full days of work. The two-week plan can usually be completed by shopping and doing the preliminary preparations one day and cooking the next.

Another helpful hint is to photocopy the recipes and glue them to large index cards. One woman displays the cards on the refrigerator, using magnets. That way she can easily follow the group of recipes she's preparing without having to turn pages back and forth.

If your spouse helps with the cooking, do the method together as a once-a-month project. Or you and a friend may enjoy cooking together. One day fix meals at her house for her freezer, and another day do the same at yours, or prepare the two-week cycle for both of you in one day. The company is fun, and it leaves one person to empty the trash, wipe off the counters, wash pans and chase the kids.

Furthermore, don't try to do any extra baking on the days you're doing this method. Some of the recipes call for bread dough, pastry shells and pie crust, but we recommend you buy those from the store rather than make them yourself on cook-

ing day. It's too time consuming to attempt. If you enjoy making pie crust, make it a couple of days ahead.

Finally, your day will go much easier if you feel free to take a break to tend to the children's needs, make a phone call or just sit down. Wear a supportive pair of shoes. Put on uplifting music. Crack open a kitchen window for ventilation and to let the good smells pour out.

Before you go to the store, check the grocery and staples lists for the cycle you plan to use. The staples list contains items you need but usually have on hand. Check through your cupboards, and add the missing staple items to the grocery shopping list. You'll also want to check the list of suggested freezer containers to see if you need to buy any of them.

Please feel free to use a copier to reproduce the grocery list; then write in the other staple items or containers you'll need to buy. This will make it easier for you when you go shopping. As an added help, the grocery lists for the one-month and two-week entrée plans have been categorized by sections of foods to help speed you through the supermarket.

It may seem like a staggering expense to buy the amount of food required to prepare these dinner entrées. You may want to budget ahead and set aside extra funds. Even though it costs more in the beginning you'll spend less over the course of a month, because you'll be buying in bulk, eating out less often and taking fewer trips to the supermarket.

Your shopping expedition is going to take a few hours, so make an outing of it and try to enjoy it. If you take young children along, be sure to go when everyone is well-fed and rested. It also helps to break up the trip. For example, go mid-morning to a discount food store to buy in bulk, have lunch at your favorite place, and then finish any leftover shopping at the supermarket. If a friend or family member will baby-sit the kids on shopping day, you'll accomplish more in less time.

At the supermarket, you'll probably need two shopping carts and a pen or pencil to mark off items on your list as you buy them. You can also save time by picking out your meat first, asking the butcher to cut it for you, and then doing the rest of your shopping while he or she prepares the meat. If your list calls for ground ham, pick out the ham, and ask the butcher to grind the end portions and save the center for dinner slices. If you need sirloin tip steak sliced in strips, choose the meat and request this help. Buy chickens four pounds or larger;

GROCERY SHOPPING HINTS

otherwise you pay for too much bone. If you can't find chickens that large, ask the butcher if any are in storage.

After you finish grocery shopping, don't bother putting away the canned and dry ingredients you'll be using on cooking day. Leave them on the dryer or on a table or counter out of the way, because you'll need them soon. You may want to stack the same or similar items in one place, such as the canned tomato paste and sauce, and the cans of soup in another. It will be easier to find them when you're preparing the entrées.

Label foods you won't need until you serve the entrées. That will remind you not to use them early. For example, place an X in black marker across a soup label, package of rice or spaghetti or on a plastic bag with a fresh tomato in it. Then put those items away.

MORE MONEY-SAVING AND SHOPPING TIPS

You can save substantially on your food bill by using *Once-a-Month Cooking* and by employing these budget-stretching tips:

First, you save the most money if you shop from a carefully prepared list. It takes superhuman strength, especially if you have your spouse and children along, not to toss a few impulse items into the basket. You've probably noticed that staple items, such as meat, produce, dairy products and bread, are shelved along the sides and back walls of the store. To get to the necessities, you have to walk past tempting convenience foods, such as chips, sodas, frozen dinners and sugared cereals. Colorful cereal boxes with free-bies are placed at children's-eye level so they'll pester you into buying them.

Second, you save more money when you make fewer trips to the store. Once you have your entrées in the freezer, you've done a major portion of your food preparation for the month. Now you can go to the supermarket less often and at a convenient time, since you won't have to buy something quick for dinner. If you plan ahead, you won't need to run to the store for "just a dozen eggs" and wind up buying two bags of groceries. For those smaller, once-a-week trips for fresh produce, bread, milk and eggs, you will also save money if you prepare a list and stick to it.

Third, you can save by buying in bulk, shopping the specials, and using coupons. When you use the once-a-month method, watch for sales on the items you need. If you go to stores that offer double the money off per coupon, you'll also save substantially.

After you've returned from grocery shopping, clear off the kitchen counters, removing any appliances or whatnots you won't be using. Then, following the "Equipment Needed for Cooking Day" list, you might want to pull out your blender, food processor, mixer, bowls or other tools you will need. If you have room on the counter, you may also want to get out the spices, condiments and staple items.

Make sure you have all needed groceries on hand. Then do the tasks outlined in the assembly order for the day before cooking day. If you don't have a food processor to chop and slice the vegetables, you may want to cut them up the day before cooking since this is one of the most time-consuming tasks. Then store vegetables (except mushrooms) in the refrigerator in cold water inside tightly sealed plastic containers. Omit the water if you put them in sealed, self-locking bags.

Finally, check over the list of freezer containers, and get out the ones you'll need. You may also want to have a quart jar on hand in case you want to save leftovers to make soup. You can usually store the meals in freezer bags unless they're layered entrées like lasagna or contain a lot of liquid. Food stored in a freezer bag can be thawed in the bag and then warmed in a suitable container.

THE DAY BEFORE COOKING DAY

The assembly order is a step-by-step outline of how to prepare all the entrées. It helps to read through the plan before you start to cook. Since you will usually be working on more than one recipe at a time, you'll be better prepared and have a sense of how the steps flow together.

The following suggestions will help make this method work best for you:

Place an empty trash can in the center of the kitchen, and keep the pets elsewhere. You'll want to prevent wasted motion wherever possible on cooking day.

Use a timer or two to remind you something is in the oven or boiling for a certain length of time. Or use a note pad to jot down when an entrée will be done.

Pause to wash pots and pans as necessary. Washing dishes and wiping up as you work will make your cleanup at the end of the day much easier.

If you have to sauté several food items in succession, use the same skillet. Sometimes you'll just need to wipe it out and put in the next ingredients. If you need an additional burner, use an electric skillet or pan. It also helps to use a crockpot overnight for the brisket, for example, and then for stew or soup on cooking day.

Set frequently used spices along the back of the stove or a nearby counter. Use one set of measuring cups and spoons for

COOKING DAY

wet ingredients and another for dry; that way you'll need to wash them less often.

Perform all similar tasks at once. For example, do all the grating, chopping and slicing of the carrots, celery, cheese and onions. Set them aside in separate bowls or plastic bags. Cook all the chickens if you didn't do that the day before. Brown all the ground beef and sauté all the onions at one time. Doing all those tasks may seem tedious, but you will have accomplished a lot when you're finished, and assembling the dishes will go much faster.

At the end of your cooking day, use leftover sliced or diced vegetables and meat for a soup, on a salad or for snacks.

FOOD STORAGE AND FREEZER TIPS

Put each dish aside on a table to cool when you've finished preparing it. When several entrées have cooled, label each with the name of the meal, date prepared and cooking instructions so you won't have to consult the recipe when it's thawed. For example: Aztec Quiche, Oct. 18. Bake uncovered 40-50 minutes at 325°.

If the recipe calls for cheese to be sprinkled on top of an entrée when you do the final preparations, put the grated cheese in a small freezer bag. Then tape the bag to the side or top of that meal's freezer container.

Make the best use of your 13x9x2-inch baking dishes. Spray a dish with nonstick spray, line the dish with heavy aluminum foil, seal the entrée and freeze it. When the entrée has frozen completely, remove it in the foil and return it to the freezer right away.

This will free your dishes and take less space in the freezer. If you don't have enough dishes, use disposable aluminum pans. They're especially nice for dishes you might like to take to someone's home or for a picnic or potluck.

When sealing food for freezing, remove as much air from the container as possible, and seal it airtight. That will help guard against freezer burn.

Post the menu of foods you've prepared on your freezer or cupboard door to help you choose each day's dinner and to keep an inventory of what entrées you've used. Check off the dishes as you serve them. And to be safe and for the freshest taste, use up the meals within a month to six weeks. (For additional freezer storage tips, see chapter 8.)

Remember each evening to pull the next night's entrée from the freezer and put it in the refrigerator to thaw. Or thaw the dish in the microwave the next day. Use the rule of thumb that by nine in the morning you'll have decided what you'll serve for dinner that night.

Each recipe includes suggestions for salads or vegetables you might serve with the entrée. You'll find some of those recipes in chapter 6, as well as a few others that go nicely with those meals. Now that you've saved time on your entrées, try some new salads, vegetables or desserts—whether you have company or the same familiar faces around your table.

Once you've prepared your first batch of meals, committed your dinner entrées to the freezer and cleaned up, go out for dinner! Sure you've got food ready, but you've just spent the day in the kitchen.

Now you'll be spending less time in the kitchen during the coming weeks because you've redeemed time, money and energy that you can invest in other rewarding ways. Time for your husband, your children and yourself. Time to have fun and entertain calmly.

Let's get cooking!

SERVING SUGGESTIONS

EQUIPMENT NEEDED FOR COOKING DAY

On cooking day, you'll want to reuse bowls and pans as much as possible to conserve counter and stove-top space. The following equipment will be needed:

Appliances
Blender or hand mixer (month one plan)
Crockpot (month one and two plans)
Food processor or grater

Pots, Pans and Skillets
1 extra large pot, canning kettle or 2 large pots (to cook chickens)
2 large pots, one with lid
1 large saucepan with lid
1 medium saucepan with lid
1 small saucepan
1 large skillet
1 medium skillet
1 rimmed baking sheet (month two plan); 2 rimmed baking sheets (low-fat plan)

Bowls and Containers
1 set of large, medium and small mixing bowls
8 to 12 small-to-medium bowls or plastic bags (for grated, sliced or chopped ingredients)

Miscellaneous Tools
Can opener
Colander
Cutting board
Hot pads
Kitchen scissors
Knives (cutting and paring)
Ladle
2 sets measuring cups (one for wet ingredients and one for dry)
2 sets measuring spoons
Metal or plastic serving spatula
Mixing spoons
Rolling pin
Rubber gloves (for deboning chicken and mixing food)
Rubber spatula
Tongs
Vegetable peeler
Wire whisk

CHAPTER 2

"For God, who gives seed to the farmer to plant, and later on, good crops to harvest and eat, will give you more and more seed to plant and will make it grow so that you can give away more and more fruit from your harvest"

(2 Corinthians 9:10, TLB).

MENU CALENDAR

SUN.	MON.	TUES.	WED.	THURS.	FRI.	SAT.
	1 Eat Out Cooking Day!	**2** Chicken Packets	**3** Mexican Stroganoff	**4** French Bread Pizza	**5** Calzones	**6** Chili Verde
7 Spaghetti	**8** Wild Rice Chicken	**9** Balkan Meatballs	**10** Marinated Flank Steak	**11** Chicken Broccoli	**12** Linguine à la Anne	**13** Chili Hamburgers
14 Baked Eggs	**15** Poulet de France					

GROCERY SHOPPING AND STAPLES LISTS

An asterisk (*) after an item indicates it can be stored until you cook the dish it will be served with. For example, the spaghetti noodles will not be cooked until the day you serve **Spaghetti**. Mark those items as a reminder that you will need them for an entrée.

When entrées require perishable foods to be refrigerated until served, you may want to use those dishes right away or buy the food the week you plan to prepare the dish. For example, fresh mushrooms would spoil by the end of a month.

For the two-week entrée plan, you will need these food items as well as the ones in the staples list that follows:

Canned Goods
1 4-ounce can chopped, green chilies
2 10¾-ounce cans condensed cream of mushroom soup
1 10¾-ounce can condensed cream of chicken soup
1 12-ounce can evaporated skim milk
1 8-ounce and 2 4-ounce cans mushroom stems and pieces
1 11½-ounce jar salsa*
3 28-ounce cans Italian-style or plain crushed tomatoes in puree
1 12-ounce can tomato paste
1 8-ounce can sliced water chestnuts

Grains, Noodles and Rice
4 hamburger buns
6 bread slices
1 loaf unsliced French bread (not sour dough)*
½ cup fine, dry bread crumbs

2 cups (about) seasoned croutons (1 cup croutons, ½ cup and ⅓ cup crushed crouton crumbs)
1 12-ounce package linguine
1 dozen corn tortillas*
1 8-ounce and 1 12-ounce package wide egg noodles*
8 ounces (1¼ cups) dry pinto beans
1 16-ounce package spaghetti*
1 12-ounce package seasoned bread stuffing (6 cups)
1 6¼-ounce package long grain and wild rice (Uncle Ben's Fast Cooking Long Grain and Wild Rice if available)

Frozen Foods
1 10-ounce package frozen, chopped broccoli
2 loaves frozen bread dough (Italian, French or pizza if available, other wise wheat)

Dairy Products

9 eggs
3/4 cup margarine
10 ounces (2 1/2 cups) grated, mild
cheddar cheese
10 ounces (6 ounces sliced and 4
ounces;* 1 cup, grated) mozzarella
cheese
4 ounces (1 cup) grated, low-fat
Monterey Jack cheese*
4 ounces (1 cup) grated Parmesan
cheese
2 ounces (1/2 cup) Romano cheese
1 3-ounce package cream cheese
1 8-ounce carton sour cream or low-fat
yogurt*
2 packages refrigerated crescent rolls*
7 cups milk

Meat and Poultry

10 pounds whole chickens or 8 pounds
boneless, skinless chicken breasts
1 pound boneless, skinless chicken
breasts
1 2/3 pounds cooked ham
2 pounds lean ground beef (or substitute ground turkey)
1 pound bulk Italian sausage
1 1/3 pounds flank steak
1/2 of a 3-ounce package of sliced
pepperoni*
2 pounds round steak
1/2 pound ground turkey

Produce

1 small bunch celery
8 cloves garlic
2 pounds brown or yellow onions
1 bunch fresh parsley
2 green bell peppers and 1 red bell
pepper (or 3 green bell peppers)

STAPLES LIST

Make sure you have the following
staples on hand; add those you don't
have to the above shopping list:
    ground allspice
    dried basil leaves
    bay leaves (4)
    black pepper
    cayenne pepper
    chicken bouillon cubes (4)
chili powder (2 tablespoons)
chili sauce (1/2 cup plus 1 tablespoon)
chopped chives (1/4 cup plus 1 table-
    spoon)
ground cloves
ground cumin
curry powder
all-purpose flour (1/4 cup plus 1 table-
    spoon)

ground ginger
light mayonnaise (2 cups)
minced onion
nonstick spray
ground nutmeg
dried oregano leaves
paprika
red wine vinegar (about 3/4 cup)

salt
seasoned salt
soy sauce (1/4 cup plus 1 teaspoon)
sugar
vegetable oil (1 cup)
waxed paper
Worcestershire sauce (2 teaspoons)

FREEZER CONTAINERS

The following list of freezer containers or flat baking dishes will be needed for the entrées in the two-week cycle. They're not the only containers in which you could freeze these foods, but the list gives you an idea of the size and number of containers you'll need.

10 sandwich bags:
Calzones

11 1-quart freezer bags:
Chicken Packets (2), **French Bread Pizza** (3), **Poulet de France**, **Linguine a la Anne** (2), **Calzones** (2), **Chili Verde**

6 1-gallon freezer bags:
Wild Rice Chicken, **Calzones** (2), **Balkan Meatballs**, **Chili Hamburgers**, **Marinated Flank Steak**

1 3-cup container:
French Bread Pizza

1 4-cup container:
Spaghetti Sauce

1 5-cup container:
Chili Verde

1 6-cup container:
Mexican Stroganoff

4 13x9x2-inch baking dishes:
Poulet de France, **Chicken Broccoli**, **Baked Eggs**, **Linguine à la Anne**

Heavy aluminum foil:
French Bread Pizza

1. Freeze the 4 hamburger buns in a plastic bag and the French bread in heavy foil, with the package of pepperoni taped to the foil. Refrigerate crescent rolls.

2. Cut 1 pound boneless, skinless chicken breasts into 1-inch cubes with kitchen scissors for **Chili Verdes**; refrigerate until needed.

3. In a large pot (may need two), place remaining 9 pounds of whole chickens (or 7 pounds of breasts) in about 3 quarts water, making sure they're completely covered. Heat to a boil; reduce heat. Cover and simmer until thickest pieces are done, about 45 minutes to 1 hour.

Save and refrigerate 2 cups chicken broth; discard remaining broth or use for soup.

Cool chicken until ready to handle; remove skin and debone. Cut into bite-size pieces with kitchen scissors, which are easier to use than a knife. Refrigerate chicken pieces in two plastic bags.

4. Set out appliances, bowls, canned goods, dry ingredients, freezer containers and recipes.

5. Thaw 2 loaves of frozen baking dough in the refrigerator overnight.

6. Rinse pinto beans; cover with water and soak overnight.

THE DAY BEFORE COOKING DAY

Make sure you've cleared the table and counters of unnecessary kitchenware to allow plenty of working room. It also helps to have fresh, damp washcloths and towels for wiping your hands and the cooking area. The day will go a lot smoother if you keep cleaning and organizing as you work.

Before you prepare a recipe, gather all the spices and ingredients in the assembly area to save time and steps. When you finish the recipe, remove unneeded items, and wipe off the work space.

Slightly undercook regular rice and noodles (al dente) that will be frozen. When you reheat them, they'll have a better consistency and won't turn mushy.

Before Assembling Dishes:

1. Cook and stir the bulk Italian sausage until brown in a large pot for **Spaghetti Sauce.** Take a minute after chopping the onions, garlic and parsley to complete **Spaghetti Sauce** according to recipe. Start sauce boiling on the front burner, reduce heat, and then move pan to a back burner for 2 hours of simmering.

2. Perform all the chopping, grating and slicing tasks.
Onions: Finely chop all (store in cold water in a container with a tight-fitting lid).
Garlic: Mince 8 cloves.
Parsley: Chop 1/2 cup.
Celery: Finely chop 1 1/2 cups.

Green and red bell peppers: Chop 1/4 cup plus 1 tablespoon green bell pepper; slice 1 green and 1 red pepper.
Cheddar cheese: Grate all.
Monterey Jack cheese: Grate all.
Mozzarella cheese: Grate 4 ounces; slice 6 ounces.
Croutons: Crush enough to make a 1/2 cup and 1/3 cup crumbs.

3. Spray pans or baking dishes you will need with nonstick spray (check list of freezer containers on page 22).

4. As you assemble the chicken, ham, beef and miscellaneous entrées, allow them to cool if necessary, put them in storage containers and freeze them.

Assemble Chicken Dishes

1. Skim off and discard chicken fat from 2 cups broth.

2. Start the **Chili Verde**.

3. Cook rice for **Wild Rice Chicken** according to package directions.

4. Make filling for **Chicken Packets** in a medium bowl (mixing with hands works best), put mixture in a bag, and freeze.

5. Assemble **Wild Rice Chicken**.

6. Start **Poulet de France**.

7. Start cooking 10-ounce package of frozen, chopped broccoli.

8. Finish assembling **Poulet de France**.

9. Assemble **Chicken Broccoli**.

10. Add chicken and spices to **Chili Verde**, and simmer 10 more minutes.

11. Cool **Spaghetti Sauce,** and freeze as directed.

12. Freeze chicken dishes.

Assemble Ham Dishes

1. Dice 1²⁄₃ pounds ham, placing 4 cups in one bowl and 1 cup in another.

2. Boil linguine according to package directions.

3. Assemble **Baked Eggs**.

4. Complete **Linguine à la Anne**.

5. Freeze ham dishes.

Assemble Beef Dishes

1. Prepare **Calzones**, and freeze.

2. Cut round steak in bite-size pieces.

3. Combine ingredients for **Mexican Stroganoff**, and start it simmering.

4. Assemble and broil **Balkan Meatballs**.

5. Prepare **Marinated Flank Steak**.

6. Prepare **Chili Hamburger** patties.

7. Freeze beef dishes.

RECIPES FOR THE TWO-WEEK ENTRÉE PLAN

Each recipe offers complete instructions on how to prepare the dish. Food items with an asterisk (*) won't be prepared until you serve the entrée. For recipes calling for oven baking, preheat oven for about 10 minutes.

"Summary of processes" gives a quick overview of foods that need to be chopped, diced, grated or sliced. "Freeze in" tells what bags and containers will be needed to freeze each entrée. "Serve with" offers suggestions of foods to accompany the meal. Some of the recipes for those foods are included in chapter 6; page numbers are indicated for easy reference. "Note" includes special instructions on how the entrée can be used in other ways.

1 pound bulk Italian sausage	4 bay leaves
1 1/2 cups finely chopped onion	2 tablespoons sugar
1 12-ounce can tomato paste	4 teaspoons dried basil leaves
3 28-ounce cans Italian-style or	2 teaspoons dried oregano leaves
plain crushed tomatoes in puree	4 tablespoons chopped fresh parsley
2 cups water	2 teaspoons salt
4 teaspoons minced garlic (4 cloves)	1 16-ounce package spaghetti*

SPAGHETTI SAUCE

In a large pot, cook and stir the bulk Italian sausage with the onion until the meat is brown; drain fat. Add remaining ingredients, except the spaghetti. Bring sauce to a boil; reduce heat. Partly cover, and simmer for 2 hours, stirring occasionally. (If desired, simmer in a crockpot instead of pot.) Makes 12 cups sauce.

After sauce has cooled, freeze 4 cups for **Spaghetti** and 3 cups for **French Bread Pizza**; divide remaining 5 cups sauce in half, and freeze in 2 1-quart bags for **Calzones**.

To prepare for serving **Spaghetti**, thaw sauce, and heat in a medium saucepan. Cook noodles according to package directions, drain, and pour sauce over them. **Makes 6 servings**.

Summary of processes: Chop 1 1/2 cups onion, 4 tablespoons parsley; mince 4 cloves garlic

Freeze in: 4-cup container, **Spaghetti**; 3-cup container, **French Bread Pizza**; 2 1-quart freezer bags, **Calzones**

Serve with: Fresh Baked Asparagus (page 145), garlic bread

FRENCH BREAD PIZZA

1 loaf unsliced French bread (not sour dough)*

3 cups Spaghetti Sauce*

1/4 cup grated Parmesan cheese*

1 cup grated mozzarella cheese*

3 ounces pepperoni slices (half a package)*

This recipe is assembled on the day it's served. Put sauce in a 3-cup container, cheeses in 2 1-quart bags, pepperoni in 1-quart bag; wrap bread in heavy foil. Freeze them together.

To prepare for serving, thaw French bread, sauce, grated cheeses and pepperoni. Slice loaf of French bread in half lengthwise. Layer sauce, Parmesan cheese, pepperoni and mozzarella cheese on each half. Set oven to broil and/or 550°. Place bread on baking sheet, and put in oven. Broil until mozzarella is melted. Cut pizza into serving-sized pieces. **Makes 6 to 8 servings.**

Summary of processes: Grate 4 ounces mozzarella cheese

Freeze in: 3-cup container; 3 1-quart bags; foil for bread

Serve with: Waldorf salad

8 ounces dry pinto beans (1¼ cups)
1 pound boneless, skinless chicken
  breasts (2 cups cooked)
1 4-ounce can chopped green chilies
1 teaspoon ground cumin
¾ teaspoon dried oregano leaves
⅛ teaspoon ground cloves
⅛ teaspoon cayenne pepper
3 cups water

3 chicken bouillon cubes
1 teaspoon minced garlic (1 clove)
1 teaspoon salt
⅔ cup finely chopped onion
1 cup grated low-fat Monterey Jack
  cheese*
1 dozen corn tortillas*
1 11½-ounce jar salsa*

CHILI VERDE

Rinse pinto beans, soak them in cold water overnight, then drain them. Cut chicken into 1-inch cubes; cook until no longer pink in small amount of water. Combine chicken with chilies and seasonings; refrigerate until needed. At the same time, combine beans, water, bouillon cubes, garlic, salt and onion in a large pot; bring to a boil. Reduce heat and simmer until beans are soft, about 1 hour. Add more water if necessary.

Combine chicken and spices with beans; simmer 10 more minutes. Cool and freeze. Grate cheese, put in a 1-quart bag, and attach it to the freezer container with the chili.

To serve, thaw chili and cheese. Simmer chili 30 minutes, stirring occasionally. Top chili with salsa and grated cheese; serve on warmed corn tortillas. **Makes 5 servings**.

Summary of processes: Soak ½ pound pinto beans overnight; chop 2 cups cooked chicken; ⅔ cup onion; grate 1 cup low-fat Monterey Jack cheese

Freeze in: 5-cup container; 1-quart bag

Serve with: Tossed green salad

WILD RICE CHICKEN

1 6¼-ounce package quick-cooking, long grain and wild rice

1 cup cooked, chopped chicken

1 8-ounce can sliced water chestnuts, drained

1 cup finely chopped celery

1¼ cups finely chopped onion

1 cup light mayonnaise*

1 10¾-ounce can condensed cream of mushroom soup*

Cook rice according to package directions. Combine rice with chopped chicken, water chestnuts, celery and onion; put mixture in a 1-gallon freezer bag.

To prepare for serving, thaw rice and chicken mixture, remove from bag, and place in a 2½ quart baking dish. Stir mayonnaise and condensed cream of mushroom soup together, and spread over top of chicken. Bake covered in a preheated 325° oven for 1 hour. **Makes 6 servings.**

Summary of processes: Chop 1 cup cooked chicken, 1 cup celery and 1¼ cups onion

Freeze in: 1-gallon bag

Serve with: Cooked green beans, peach halves with cottage cheese topped with a maraschino cherry, and **Blueberry Pie** (page 140)

2 cups cooked, chopped chicken
1 3-ounce package cream cheese, softened
1 tablespoon chopped chives
2 tablespoons milk
Salt to taste

¹/₂ cup crushed, seasoned crouton
   crumbs*
2 packages refrigerated crescent rolls*
¹/₄ cup melted margarine*

Mix chicken, cream cheese, chives, milk and salt in a medium bowl (mixing with hands works best) to make filling, and store in a 1-quart freezer bag. Put crouton crumbs in another 1-quart bag, attach it to bag of chicken filling, and freeze them. Refrigerate crescent rolls.

To prepare for serving, thaw chicken mixture. Unroll crescent rolls. Each tube will contain 4 rectangles of dough with a diagonal perforation. Press dough along each perforation so the rectangle halves will not separate. Place about ¹/₄ cup of chicken mixture into the center of each rectangle. Fold dough over the filling, and pinch the edges to seal tightly. Dip each packet in melted margarine, and coat with crouton crumbs. Place packets on a baking sheet. Bake in a preheated 350° oven for 20 minutes or until golden brown. Packets are good either hot or cold. (Serve early in the month before date expires on crescent rolls.) **Makes 8 packets.**

Summary of processes: Chop 2 cups cooked chicken and 1 tablespoon chives

Freeze in: 2 1-quart bags

Serve with: Smoky Corn Chowder (page 144), baked apples stuffed with plump raisins

Note: These packets are a favorite with children.

POULET DE FRANCE

1 12-ounce package seasoned bread stuffing (6 cups)

2 tablespoons melted margarine

2 cups chicken broth

3 cups chopped, cooked chicken

1/2 cup finely chopped onion

1/4 cup minced chives

1/2 cup finely chopped celery

1/2 cup light mayonnaise

3/4 teaspoon salt

2 eggs

1 1/2 cups milk

1 10 3/4-ounce can condensed cream of mushroom soup

1/2 cup grated mild cheddar cheese

In a medium bowl, mix stuffing, melted margarine and 1 1/4 cups broth. Mix chicken, 3/4 cup broth, onion, chives, celery, mayonnaise and salt in another bowl.

Spread half the stuffing in a 13x9x2-inch baking dish treated with nonstick spray. Spread chicken mixture over stuffing. Cover with remaining stuffing. Whisk eggs, milk and soup in a large bowl. Pour sauce evenly over stuffing. Cover dish with foil, and freeze. Put cheese in a small freezer bag, and attach it to dish.

To prepare for serving, thaw grated cheese and chicken dish. Bake covered in a pre-heated 325° oven for 30 minutes. Remove foil, sprinkle with cheese, and continue to bake uncovered for 10 minutes more. **Makes 8 servings.**

Summary of processes: Chop 3 cups cooked chicken, 1/2 cup onions and 1/2 cup celery; mince 1/4 cup chives; grate 1/2 cup mild cheddar cheese

Freeze in: 13x9x2-inch baking dish; 1-quart bag

Serve with: Cooked frozen peas, lemon gelatin with pears, **Cranberry Tea** (page 139)

Note: This is a super dish to take to a potluck dinner.

1 10-ounce package frozen, chopped broccoli
4 cups cooked, chopped chicken
1 10 3/4-ounce can condensed cream of chicken soup

1/2 cup low-fat mayonnaise
1 4-ounce can mushroom stems and pieces, drained
1/4 teaspoon curry powder
3/4 cup grated Parmesan cheese

Cook broccoli in boiling water according to package directions. Drain broccoli, and spread it in a 13x9x2-inch baking dish. Mix chicken, soup, mayonnaise, mushrooms, curry powder and 1/2 cup Parmesan cheese in a medium bowl. Spread chicken mixture over broccoli. Sprinkle 1/4 cup Parmesan cheese over top. Cover dish with foil, and freeze.

To prepare for serving, thaw dish, and bake covered in a preheated 350° oven for 40 minutes. Remove foil, stir to bring colder food in center to the outside; bake 20 minutes more. **Makes 6 servings.**

Summary of processes: Chop 4 cups cooked chicken

Freeze in: 13x9x2-inch baking dish

Serve with: Croissants, **Cranberry Cream Salad** (page 142)

6 bread slices, cut in cubes
2 cups grated mild cheddar cheese
1 cup cooked, cubed ham
1/4 cup chopped green bell pepper

1/2 cup finely chopped onion
6 eggs
3 cups milk

Mix bread, cheese, ham, bell pepper and onion; spread in a 13x9x2-inch baking dish treated with nonstick spray. Whisk eggs and milk, and pour over top. Cover dish with foil and freeze.

To prepare for serving, thaw dish, and bake uncovered in a preheated 375° oven for 45 minutes. **Makes 8 to 10 servings.**

Summary of processes: Cut bread and ham into cubes; grate 2 cups mild cheddar cheese; chop 1/4 cup green bell pepper and 1/2 cup onion

Freeze in: 13x9x2-inch baking dish

Serve with: Hot Spiced Fruit (page 143)

Note: This dish is good with 6 slices cooked, crumbled bacon instead of ham. You can also make this dish the night before, refrigerate it, and serve it the next morning. It's nice for company brunch after church.

LINGUINE À LA ANNE

1 12-ounce package linguine
2 tablespoons margarine
2 tablespoons all-purpose flour
1/2 teaspoon salt
1 12-ounce can evaporated skim milk
1 4-ounce can mushroom stems and pieces, save liquid
1 1/3 cups water

1 chicken bouillon cube
4 cups cooked, cubed ham
1/2 cup grated Romano cheese
1 sliced red bell pepper
1 sliced green bell pepper
1 tablespoon vegetable oil
1 cup seasoned croutons*

Cook linguine in a large pot according to package directions, drain, and return to pot. While linguine cooks, melt margarine in a medium saucepan over low heat. Stir in flour and salt, adding evaporated milk. Bring to a boil, stirring constantly. Boil and stir 1 minute. Add liquid from mushrooms, water and boullion cube. Cook over medium heat, stirring constantly, until bubbly and slightly thickened.

Add 2 cups sauce and drained mushrooms to linguine, and toss until well mixed. Spoon linguine mixture into a 13x9x2-inch baking dish, pressing it up the sides to leave a slight hollow in center of dish.

Toss ham in remaining sauce; spread it in the center of the linguine. Sprinkle with Romano cheese; cover with foil, and freeze dish. Sauté red and green bell peppers in vegetable oil until soft; allow to cool. Put peppers in 1-quart freezer bag; attach this bag and croutons in a 1-quart freezer bag to the dish.

To prepare for serving, thaw dish, peppers and croutons. Bake dish uncovered in a preheated 400° oven for 20 minutes. Before serving, sprinkle croutons around edge of casserole. Reheat sautéed red and green bell peppers, and mound them in the center.
Makes 8 servings.

Summary of processes: Cut ham into cubes; slice 1 red bell pepper and 1 green bell pepper

Freeze in: 13x9x2-inch baking dish; 2 1-quart bags

Serve with: Cooked zucchini, **Orange Spiced Tea** (page 139)

Note: Great for company that includes children.

2 loaves frozen bread dough (Italian, French or pizza)

6 ounces sliced mozzarella cheese
5 cups Spaghetti Sauce

Thaw two loaves of bread dough. Divide each loaf into 5 parts each. One at a time, roll each dough piece on a floured board or stretch with your hands, making 10 7-inch squares. Fold each dough square over half a cheese slice to form a turnover, and pinch edges to seal. (You can also ladle 1/3 cup to 1/2 cup sauce onto center of each square before making the turnover, but the sauce tends to seep out.)

Place each turnover in a small sandwich bag. Put 5 turnovers in a 1-gallon freezer bag. Divide sauce in half, and store in 2 1-quart freezer bags; enclose each bag of sauce in a bag of **Calzones**. Do the same with the remaining 5 turnovers.

To prepare for serving, thaw sauce; heat in a medium pan 10 to 15 minutes until bubbly. At the same time, take frozen turnovers out of bags, and place them about 2 inches apart on a baking sheet sprayed with a nonstick spray. Preheat oven to 350°. Bake for about 15 minutes. Turnovers will be golden brown when done. Ladle sauce on top of turnovers, and serve. **Makes 10 servings.**

Freeze in: 2 1-gallon bags; 2 1-quart bags; 10 sandwich bags

Serve with: Tossed salad with Italian dressing

Note: All ages love these! They're convenient, since you can bake only as many as needed at a time.

MEXICAN STROGANOFF

2 pounds round steak
1 cup finely chopped onion
2 teaspoons minced garlic (2 cloves)
2 tablespoons vegetable oil
1/3 cup red wine vinegar
1 3/4 cups water
1/2 cup chili sauce
1 tablespoon paprika
1 tablespoon chili powder

2 teaspoons seasoned salt
1 teaspoon soy sauce
1 8-ounce can mushroom stems and
  pieces, drained
1 8-ounce carton sour cream or low-fat
  yogurt*
3 tablespoons all-purpose flour*
1 12-ounce package wide egg noodles*

Cut steak into bite-size pieces. Cook and stir steak, onion and garlic in oil in a large saucepan over medium heat until brown. Drain off oil. Stir vinegar, water, chili sauce, paprika, chili powder, seasoned salt, soy sauce and mushrooms into steak mixture. Bring to a boil; reduce heat. Cover and simmer 1 hour until meat is tender. Cool and store in freezer container.

To prepare for serving, thaw meat mixture and heat in saucepan until bubbly. Cook egg noodles according to package directions. Stir sour cream or low-fat yogurt and flour together; combine with stroganoff. Heat to a boil, stirring constantly. Reduce heat; simmer and stir about 1 minute. Serve stroganoff over noodles. **Makes 6 to 8 servings.**

Summary of processes: Cut steak in bite-size pieces; chop 1 cup onion; mince 2 cloves garlic

Freeze in: 6-cup container

Serve with: Tomatoes stuffed with guacamole, corn on the cob

1 egg
1/4 cup milk
1/3 cup crushed seasoned croutons
3/4 teaspoon salt
3/4 teaspoon sugar
1/4 teaspoon ground ginger
1/4 teaspoon ground nutmeg
1/4 teaspoon ground allspice

1 pound lean ground beef
1/2 pound ground turkey
2/3 cup finely chopped onion
1 8-ounce package wide egg noodles*
2 tablespoons margarine*
1/4 cup all-purpose flour*
2 cups milk*
Parsley for garnish*

BALKAN MEATBALLS

In a medium-size mixing bowl, beat egg with milk. Mix in the crushed croutons, salt, sugar and spices. Add beef, turkey and onion; mix thoroughly. Shape meat mixture into meatballs the size of walnuts. Place meatballs on a rimmed cookie sheet; broil until lightly browned. Cool; put meatballs in a large bag, and freeze them.

To prepare for serving, thaw meatballs. Cook noodles according to package directions. At the same time, make white sauce in a large skillet. Melt margarine over low heat. Add flour, stirring constantly until mixture is smooth and bubbly. Gradually stir in milk. Heat to boiling over medium heat, stirring constantly. Boil and stir 1 minute until thick and smooth. Add meatballs to sauce. Bring to a boil; reduce heat. Cover pan; simmer 15 minutes, stirring occasionally. Serve meatballs and sauce over wide egg noodles. Chop parsley; sprinkle over top. **Makes 4 servings.**

Summary of processes: Chop 2/3 cup onion

Freeze in: 1-gallon bag

Serve with: Cooked, fresh broccoli, **Portuguese Sweet Bread** (page 134)

MARINATED FLANK STEAK

½ cup vegetable oil
¼ cup soy sauce
¼ cup red wine vinegar
2 teaspoons Worcestershire sauce
½ teaspoon ground ginger
1 teaspoon minced garlic (1 clove)
1⅓ pounds flank steak

Mix first six ingredients for marinade. Put flank steak in a freezer bag, pour marinade over it, seal bag, and freeze.

To prepare for serving, thaw flank steak, remove from marinade, and barbecue 8 to 10 minutes per side; or set oven control to broil and/or 550°. Broil steak 6 inches from heat until brown, turning once, about 6 minutes on one side and 4 minutes on the other. Cut steak across grain at slanted angle into thin slices. **Makes 4 servings.**

Summary of processes: Mince 1 clove garlic

Freeze in: 1-gallon bag

Serve with: **Twice-Baked Potatoes Deluxe** (page 145), cooked zucchini

CHILI HAMBURGERS

1 pound lean ground beef or turkey
2 tablespoons finely chopped green bell pepper
1 tablespoon minced onion
1 tablespoon chili powder
1 tablespoon chili sauce
¼ teaspoon black pepper
½ teaspoon salt
4 hamburger buns*

Thoroughly mix all ingredients except hamburger buns. Shape into 4 hamburger patties. Freeze in a large freezer bag, with waxed paper between each one.

To prepare for serving, thaw patties and hamburger buns. Grill or fry patties to desired pinkness in center. Serve on warmed hamburger buns. **Makes 4 servings.**

Summary of processes: Chop 2 tablespoons green bell pepper

Freeze in: 1-gallon bag

Serve with: French fries or baked beans, **Jiffy Salad** (page 142)

CHAPTER 3

"She is like the merchant ships, bringing her food from afar. She gets up while it is still dark; she provides food for her family and portions for her servant girls"

(Proverbs 31:14-15, NIV).

MENU CALENDAR

SUN.	MON.	TUES.	WED.	THURS.	FRI.	SAT.
	1 Eat Out Cooking Day!	**2** Manicotti	**3** Chinese Chicken Morsels	**4** Veal Scaloppine in Spaghetti Sauce	**5** Teriyaki Burgers	**6** Ham and Swiss Pastry Bake
7 Baked Eggs	**8** Cheesy Corn Casserole	**9** Poulet de France	**10** Mimi's Chicken Soup	**11** Joes to Go	**12** Ham Loaf	**13** Barbecued Fillets
14 Meal-in-One Potatoes	**15** Hot Brisket Sandwiches	**16** Spaghetti	**17** Chicken Packets	**18** Aztec Quiche	**19** Wild Rice Chicken	**20** Taco Pie
21 Linguine à la Anne	**22** Stove-Top Barbecued Chicken	**23** French Bread Pizza	**24** Ham Dinner Slices	**25** Ravioli Soup	**26** Heavenly Chicken	**27** Mrs. Ringle's Brisket
28 Baked Herb Fish Fillets	**29** Teriyaki Chicken	**30** Fruity Curried Chicken				

GROCERY SHOPPING AND STAPLES LISTS

An asterisk (*) after an item indicates that it can be stored until you cook the dish it will be served with. For example, the spaghetti noodles will not be cooked until the day you serve **Spaghetti**. Mark those items as a reminder that you'll need them for an entrée.

When entrées require perishable foods to be refrigerated until served, you may want to use those dishes right away or buy the food the week you plan to prepare the dish. For example, fresh mushrooms would spoil by the end of a month.

For the month one entrée plan, you will need these food items as well as the ones in the staples list that follows:

GROCERY SHOPPING LIST

Canned Goods
1 8³/4-ounce can apricots
1 14¹/2-ounce can beef broth
1 8-ounce bottle chili sauce
2 10³/4-ounce cans condensed cream of mushroom soup (1 can)*
1 12-ounce can evaporated skim milk
2 4-ounce cans diced, green chilies
1 8³/4-ounce can red kidney beans
1 17-ounce can whole kernel corn
1 2-ounce and 1 4-ounce can mushroom stems and pieces
4 28-ounce cans Italian-style or plain crushed tomatoes in puree
1 12-ounce and 1 6-ounce can tomato paste
3 8-ounce cans tomato sauce
1 8-ounce can sliced water chestnuts

Grains, Pasta and Rice
7 bread slices
1 loaf unsliced French bread (not sour dough)*
6 hamburger buns*
8 to 10 sandwich rolls*
1 8-ounce container Italian-flavored bread crumbs*
1 12-ounce package linguine
1 8-ounce package manicotti
1 16-ounce package spaghetti*
1 8-ounce package spinach or wide egg noodles*
1 8-ounce package tortellini*
1 12-ounce package seasoned bread stuffing (6 cups)

41

1 6¼-ounce package long grain and wild rice (Uncle Ben's Fast Cooking Long Grain and Wild Rice if available)

1 32-ounce package regular rice

Dry Ingredients and Seasonings

⅓ cup raisins

1 package onion soup mix

1 envelope taco seasoning mix

1½ cups (about) seasoned croutons (1 cup croutons, ½ cup crushed)

Frozen Foods

4 frozen fish fillets (about 1¼ pounds) orange roughy or sole

2 9-inch deep-dish frozen pie shells (1*)

1 12-ounce package plain ravioli with out sauce* (located in the frozen or refrigerated section)

1 10-ounce package frozen, chopped spinach

Dairy Products

1 cup (about) margarine

1 8-ounce carton small curd, low-fat cottage cheese with chives

1 16-ounce carton small curd, low-fat cottage cheese

2 packages refrigerated crescent rolls*

21 eggs

1 cup half-and-half

2 quarts plus ½ cup and 1 tablespoon milk

18 ounces (4½ cups) grated, mild cheddar cheese

1 3-ounce package cream cheese

5 ounces (1¼ cups) grated Monterey Jack cheese

16 ounces (4 cups) mozzarella cheese (4 slices, remaining grated)

12 ounces (about 3 cups) grated Parmesan cheese

1 15-ounce container part-skim ricotta cheese

2 ounces (½ cup) grated Romano cheese

4 ounces (1 cup) grated Swiss cheese

1 8-ounce carton sour cream

Meat and Poultry

1 4-to-6-pound beef brisket

7¾ pounds lean ground beef (This allows 1 pound for hamburgers; buy more if needed for your family.)

½ pound freshly ground turkey

9 pounds whole chickens or 7 pounds breasts

5¾ pounds boneless, skinless chicken breasts

2 pounds chicken pieces (breasts, drumsticks or thighs)

4 strips bacon

6 to 7 pounds boneless, cooked ham, with 3 pounds cubed, 1½ pounds ground from the two ends and the center portion cut in dinner slices

1 pound bulk Italian sausage

1 pound very thin, boneless veal cut
lets* (or substitute 1 pound boneless,
skinless chicken breasts)
3-ounce package (use ¹/₂) sliced pepperoni

Produce
3 medium carrots
1 bunch celery
1 whole head garlic (9¹/₂ cloves)

1 small lemon*
1 small head of lettuce
1 small bunch green onions
3 medium, green bell peppers (or 2
medium, green bell peppers and 1
medium, red bell pepper)
2¹/₂ pounds (about 7) yellow onions
1 bunch fresh parsley

Make sure you have the following
staples on hand; add those you don't
have to the above shopping list:
dried basil leaves
bay leaves
biscuit baking mix (1 cup)
brown sugar (about 1¹/₃ cups)
catsup (¹/₃ cup)
cayenne pepper
celery seeds
chicken bouillon cube
chili powder
ground cinnamon
cloves (whole)
ground cumin
curry powder
all-purpose flour
garlic powder
garlic salt
ground ginger
lemon juice (about ²/₃ cup)
8 medium baking potatoes*

8 to 10 new potatoes*
3 tomatoes*
lemon pepper
light mayonnaise (about 2 cups)
minced onion
Dijon mustard (¹/₄ cup)
Dried mustard (1 teaspoon)
Prepared mustard (about ¹/₂ cup)
nonstick spray
onion salt
dried oregano leaves
pepper
salt
soda crackers (1³/₄ cups crumbs)
soy sauce (³/₄ cup)
sugar
dried thyme leaves
vegetable oil
red wine vinegar
white vinegar
waxed paper
Worcestershire sauce

STAPLES LIST

FREEZER CONTAINERS

The following list of freezer containers or flat baking dishes will be needed for the entrées. These are not the only containers you could use, but this list gives you an idea of the size and number of containers you'll need.

Heavy aluminum foil

15 1-quart freezer bags:
French Bread Pizza (3), **Linguine à la Anne** (2), **Chicken Packets** (2), **Veal Scaloppine in Spaghetti Sauce** (2), **Heavenly Chicken, Poulet de France, Taco Pie, Cheesy Corn Casserole, Meal-in-One Potatoes, Baked Herb Fish Fillets**

13 1-gallon freezer bags:
Mrs. Ringle's Brisket, Hot Brisket Sandwiches, Veal Scaloppine, Ham Loaf, Ham and Swiss Pastry Bake, Wild Rice Chicken, Chinese Chicken Morsels, Barbecued Fillets, Ham Dinner Slices, Teriyaki Burgers, Teriyaki Chicken, Baked Herb Fish Fillets, Stove-Top Barbecued Chicken

1 4-cup container:
Spaghetti Sauce

2 3-cup containers:
Veal Scaloppine in Spaghetti Sauce, French Bread Pizza

1 4-cup container:
Fruity Curried Chicken

3 8-cup containers:
Ravioli Soup, Joes to Go, Mimi's Chicken Soup

2 8x8x2-inch baking dishes:
Cheesy Corn Casserole, Baked Eggs

3 13x9x2-inch baking dishes:
Linguine à la Anne, Heavenly Chicken, Poulet de France

1 3-quart casserole of any shape:
Manicotti

1 9-inch quiche or pie pan:
Aztec Quiche

1 10-inch quiche or pie pan:
Taco Pie

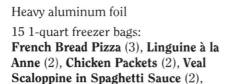

1. Cut 1½ pounds of boneless chicken breasts into 1-inch cubes with kitchen scissors and refrigerate. Refrigerate remaining boneless chicken breasts and 2 pounds of chicken pieces.

2. Refrigerate lemon, and store baking and new potatoes until you're ready to serve them.

3. Place 9 pounds whole chickens (or 7 pounds breasts) in about 6 quarts water in a large pot (may need two). Bring to a boil; reduce heat. Cover and simmer until thickest pieces are done, about 45 minutes to 1 hour. Save and refrigerate 3¼ quarts chicken broth.

   Cool chicken until ready to handle. Remove meat from bones and skin. Cut chicken into bite-size pieces using kitchen scissors, which are easier to use than a knife. Refrigerate chicken pieces in two plastic bags.

4. Put ham dinner slices, hamburger buns and sandwich rolls in freezer bags; mark bags with names of recipes; store them in freezer until you're ready to serve them.

5. For **Veal Scaloppine in Spaghetti Sauce,** put veal cutlets in 1-gallon bag, Italian-flavored bread crumbs and mozzarella cheese in separate 1-quart bags; freeze them together.

6. For **French Bread Pizza**, put pepperoni in 1-quart freezer bag, ¼ cup grated Parmesan cheese and 1 cup grated mozzarella cheese in separate 1-quart freezer bags; wrap French bread in heavy foil, and put them together in freezer.

7. Set out appliances, bowls, canned goods, dry ingredients, freezer containers and recipes.

8. Start **Mrs. Ringle's Brisket** in a crockpot (just before bed).

COOKING DAY ASSEMBLY ORDER

Make sure you've cleared the table and counters of unnecessary kitchenware to allow plenty of working room. It also helps to have fresh, damp washcloths and towels for wiping your hands and the cooking area. The day will go a lot smoother if you keep cleaning and organizing as you work.

Before you prepare a recipe, gather all the spices and ingredients in the assembly area to save time and steps. When you finish the recipe, remove unneeded items, and wipe off the work space.

Before Assembling Dishes:

1. Cool, slice and divide brisket and gravy in half for **Mrs. Ringle's Brisket** and **Hot Brisket Sandwiches**. Put brisket in two 1-gallon bags, and freeze them. Wash out crockpot.

2. Skim and discard fat from chicken broth.

3. Perform all chopping, crushing, grating and slicing tasks.
Ham: Cut 8 cups into cubes; grind 1 1/2 pounds (if the butcher didn't do this).
Onions: Leave one onion whole for **Mimi's Chicken Soup**; finely chop remaining onions. Open windows, and keep tissues handy. Store onions in cold water in a container with a tight lid.
Green onions: Chop 1/2 cup.
Green bell peppers: Finely chop 1; slice 1.
Red bell pepper: Slice 1.
Carrots: Shred 3.
Celery: Slice 1/2 cup with leaves; finely chop 1 3/4 cups.
Garlic: Mince 8 1/2 teaspoons (8 1/2 cloves).
Parsley: Chop 2/3 cup.
Mozzarella cheese: Cut 4 slices; grate the rest.
Monterey Jack cheese: Grate all.
Mild cheddar cheese: Grate all.
Cracker crumbs: Crush 1 3/4 cups.

4. Start **Spaghetti Sauce**.

5. Spray pans or baking dishes you will need with nonstick spray (check list of freezer containers on page 44).

6. As you assemble the ham, chicken, beef and miscellaneous entrées, allow them to cool if necessary, put them in storage containers, and freeze them.

Assemble Ham Dishes

1. Boil linguine according to the package directions, setting timer.

2. Assemble **Ham Loaf**.

3. Finish preparing **Linguine à la Anne**.

4. Assemble **Ham and Swiss Pastry Bake**.

5. Freeze ham dishes.

Assemble Poultry Dishes

1. Prepare **Stove-Top Barbecued Chicken** in a skillet, and simmer.

2. In separate saucepans, cook rice for **Wild Rice Chicken** and the 3/4 cup regular rice for **Fruity Curried Chicken** according to package directions.

3. Make filling for **Chicken Packets** in a medium bowl (mixing with hands works best), and put in a freezer bag.

4. Finish assembling **Wild Rice Chicken** and **Fruity Curried Chicken**.

5. Prepare **Heavenly Chicken**.

6. Prepare **Chinese Chicken Morsels**.

7. Assemble **Poulet de France**.

8. Assemble filling for **Meal-in-One Potatoes**.

9. Assemble **Teriyaki Chicken**.

10. Prepare **Mimi's Chicken Soup** with remaining chicken broth, and start simmering.

11. Freeze poultry dishes.

Assemble Miscellaneous Dishes

1. Prepare **Baked Herb Fish Fillets** coating mix.

2. Complete **Aztec Quiche**.

3. Prepare **Baked Eggs**. (If you use bacon for **Baked Eggs**, at the same time you fry it, fry 5 more slices till limp, and set aside for **Barbecued Fillets**.)

4. Cool **Spaghetti Sauce**.

5. Freeze miscellaneous dishes.

Assemble Beef Dishes

1. Cook manicotti according to package directions.

2. Assemble **Teriyaki Burgers**.

3. Complete **Barbecued Fillets**.

4. Drain manicotti; rinse with cold water. Separate manicotti noodles; put each on waxed paper.

5. In a large skillet, cook and stir 5 pounds lean ground beef until brown.

6. In a small skillet, sauté 1/3 and 3/4 cups chopped onions until tender; use for **Taco Pie** and **Joes to Go.**

7. Assemble **Ravioli Soup**, starting it to simmer.

8. Finish **Manicotti**.

9. Put **Spaghetti Sauce** in freezer containers according to directions. Put containers of sauce for **Veal Scaloppine in Spaghetti Sauce** and **French Bread Pizza** in freezer with already packaged items for those dishes.

10. Assemble **Taco Pie**.

11. Prepare **Joes to Go**.

12. Complete **Cheesy Corn Casserole**.

13. Allow **Mimi's Chicken Soup** and **Ravioli Soup** to cool, and store in freezer containers.

14. Freeze beef dishes.

You made it! Hooray!!

RECIPES FOR THE MONTH ONE ENTRÉE PLAN

Each recipe offers complete instructions on how to prepare the dish. Food items with an asterisk (*) won't be prepared until you serve the entrée. For recipes calling for oven baking, preheat oven for about 10 minutes.

"Summary of processes" gives a quick overview of foods that need to be chopped, diced, grated or sliced. "Freeze in" tells what bags and containers will be needed to freeze each entrée. "Serve with" offers suggestions of foods to accompany the meal. Some of the recipes for those foods are included in chapter 6; page numbers are indicated for easy reference. "Note" includes special instructions on how the entrée can be used in other ways.

1 4-to-6 pound brisket
2 tablespoons prepared mustard

1 package onion soup mix
4 to 5 new potatoes*

Place brisket fat side up in a crockpot. Do not add any water or liquid. Cover brisket with mustard and dry onion soup mix. Cook on low overnight.

Skim mustard and onion seasoning from brisket; mix with liquid. Remove brisket from crockpot; allow to cool. Peel off fat, and discard it; slice or shred meat. Save juices and seasonings (thicken with flour to make gravy if desired). Divide meat and gravy in half, and store in separate 1-gallon bags in freezer. Reserve 1 bag for **Mrs. Ringle's Brisket** and one for **Hot Brisket Sandwiches**.

To prepare for serving, thaw brisket and gravy, and heat. At the same time, prepare new potatoes. Heat 1 cup salted water to a boil; add potatoes. Cover and heat till boiling; reduce heat. Simmer tightly covered until tender, 20 to 25 minutes; drain. Serve potatoes with brisket and gravy. **Makes 4 to 5 servings.**

Freeze in: 2 1-gallon bags

Serve with: Cheese grits, **Cranberry Cream Salad** (page 142)

Half of gravy and sliced brisket
4 to 6 sandwich rolls

Margarine or mayonnaise for rolls

Thaw brisket slices; heat them in the gravy. Serve on warm sandwich rolls. Serve gravy on the side for dipping. **Makes 4 to 6 servings**.

Serve with: Cinnamon Applesauce Salad (page 142) and celery slices

SPAGHETTI SAUCE

1 pound bulk Italian sausage
1 ½ cups finely chopped onion
1 12-ounce can tomato paste
3 28-ounce cans Italian-style or plain crushed tomatoes in puree
2 cups water
4 teaspoons minced garlic (4 cloves)

4 bay leaves
2 tablespoons sugar
4 teaspoons dried basil leaves
2 teaspoons dried oregano leaves
4 tablespoons chopped fresh parsley
2 teaspoons salt
1 16-ounce package spaghetti*

In a large pot, cook and stir the bulk Italian sausage with onions until the meat is brown; drain fat. Add remaining ingredients, except the spaghetti. Bring sauce to a boil; reduce heat. Partly cover, and simmer for 2 hours, stirring occasionally. (If desired, simmer in a crockpot instead of pot.) Makes 12 cups sauce.

Allow sauce to cool. Freeze in separate containers for **Spaghetti** (4 cups); **Veal Scaloppine in Spaghetti Sauce** (2 ½ cups); and **French Bread Pizza** (3 cups). Reserve 2 ½ cups sauce for **Manicotti**.

To prepare **Spaghetti**, thaw 4 cups sauce, and heat in a medium saucepan. At the same time, cook noodles according to package directions, drain, and pour sauce over them. **Makes 6 servings.**

Summary of processes: Chop 1½ cups onions, 4 tablespoons parsley; mince 4 cloves garlic

Freeze in: 4-cup container, **Spaghetti**; 2 3-cup containers **French Bread Pizza** and **Veal Scaloppine in Spaghetti Sauce**; reserve 2½ cups for **Manicotti**

Serve with: Jiffy Salad (page 142), garlic bread

1 pound thin veal cutlets (or substitute
1 pound boneless, skinless chicken
  breasts)*
2 ½ cups Spaghetti Sauce*
1 egg*

¾ cup Italian-flavored bread crumbs*
3 tablespoons vegetable or olive oil*
1 teaspoon minced garlic (1 clove)*
4 slices mozzarella cheese*
Grated Parmesan cheese*

VEAL SCALLOPINE IN SPAGHETTI SAUCE

    This recipe is assembled on the day it's served. Put veal cutlets in 1-gallon bag, **Spaghetti Sauce** in a 3-cup container, Italian-flavored bread crumbs and mozzarella cheese in separate 1-quart bags; freeze them together.

    Thaw veal cutlets, bread crumbs, cheese slices and container of **Spaghetti Sauce**. Beat egg with fork until white and yolk are blended. Sprinkle Italian-flavored bread crumbs on a sheet of waxed paper. Dip veal into egg and then crumbs, turning to coat both sides evenly.

    In a large skillet, heat oil with garlic over medium or medium-high heat. Add veal; sauté 4 minutes on each side, until golden brown. Top each piece of veal with a cheese slice. Pour **Spaghetti Sauce** around veal. Bring sauce to boil; reduce heat. Cover and simmer 5 minutes or until cheese is melted. Sprinkle Parmesan cheese on top. **Makes 4 servings.**

    Summary of processes: Mince 1 clove garlic; slice 4 slices mozzarella cheese

    Freeze in: 3-cup container, 1-gallon bag, and 2 1-quart bags

    Serve with: Tossed green salad, **Dawn's French Bread** (page 135)

FRENCH BREAD PIZZA

1 loaf unsliced French bread (not sour dough)*

3 cups Spaghetti Sauce*

¼ cup grated Parmesan cheese*

1 cup grated mozzarella cheese*

3 ounces pepperoni slices (half a package)*

This recipe is assembled on the day it's served. Put sauce in a 3-cup container, cheeses in 2 1-quart bags, pepperoni in 1-quart bag; wrap bread in heavy foil. Freeze them together.

To prepare for serving, thaw French bread, sauce, grated cheeses and pepperoni. Slice loaf of French bread in half lengthwise. Layer sauce, Parmesan cheese, pepperoni and mozzarella cheese on each half. Set oven to broil and/or 550°. Place bread on baking sheet, and put in the oven. Broil until mozzarella is melted. Cut into serving-sized pieces. **Makes 6 to 8 servings.**

Summary of processes: Grate 4 ounces mozzarella cheese

Freeze in: 3-cup container; 3 1-quart bags; foil for bread

Serve with: Waldorf salad

1 12-ounce package linguine
2 tablespoons margarine
2 tablespoons all-purpose flour
1/2 teaspoon salt
1 12-ounce can evaporated skim milk
1 4-ounce can mushroom stems and
pieces, save liquid
1 1/3 cups water

1 chicken bouillon cube
4 cups cooked, cubed ham
1/2 cup grated Romano cheese
1 sliced red bell pepper
1 sliced green bell pepper
1 tablespoon vegetable oil
1 cup seasoned croutons*

LINGUINE À LA ANNE

Cook linguine in a large pot according to package directions, drain, and return to pot. While linguine cooks, melt margarine in a medium saucepan over low heat. Stir in flour and salt, adding evaporated milk. Bring to a boil, stirring constantly. Boil and stir 1 minute. Add liquid from mushrooms, water and bouillon cube. Cook over medium heat, stirring constantly, until bubbly and slightly thickened.

Add 2 cups sauce and drained mushrooms to linguine, and toss until well mixed. Spoon linguine mixture into a 13x9x2-inch baking dish, pressing it up the sides to leave a slight hollow in center of dish.

Toss ham in remaining sauce; spread it in the center of the linguine. Sprinkle with Romano cheese; cover with foil, and freeze dish. Sauté red and green bell peppers in vegetable oil until soft; allow to cool. Put peppers in 1-quart freezer bag; attach this bag and croutons in a 1-quart freezer bag to the dish.

To prepare for serving, thaw dish, peppers and croutons. Bake dish uncovered in a preheated 400° oven for 20 minutes. Before serving, sprinkle croutons around edge of casserole. Reheat sautéed red and green bell peppers, and mound them in the center. **Makes 8 servings.**

Summary of processes: Cut ham into cubes; slice 1 red bell pepper and 1 green bell pepper

Freeze in: 13x9x2-inch baking dish; 2 1-quart bags

Serve with: Cooked zucchini, **Orange Spiced Tea** (page 139)

Note: Great for company that includes children.

HAM LOAF

1 1/2 pounds cooked, ground ham (3 3/4 cups)
3/4 pound lean ground beef
2 eggs

2 1/2 teaspoons prepared mustard
1/2 teaspoon salt
1 cup milk
3/4 cup crushed soda cracker crumbs

Combine ground ham, beef, eggs, mustard, salt, milk and cracker crumbs (mixing with hands works best) until well mixed. Freeze the mixture in 1-gallon freezer bag.

To prepare for serving, thaw ham loaf, remove from bag, and shape in a 9x5x3-inch loaf pan. Cover pan with foil; bake in a preheated 325° oven for 45 minutes. Carefully drain liquid. While baking, prepare sauce; spread over loaf.

HAM SAUCE

3/4 cup brown sugar*
1 tablespoon prepared mustard*
2 teaspoons water*

1 tablespoon white vinegar or lemon juice*

Stir above ingredients together; pour over loaf. Bake 30 minutes more uncovered. Baste twice. **Makes 6 servings.**

Summary of processes: Crush 3/4 cup cracker crumbs

Freeze in: 1-gallon bag

Serve with: Hot Spiced Fruit (page 143), **Twice-Baked Potatoes Deluxe** (page 145).

2 cups cooked, cubed ham
1 cup grated Swiss cheese
1/4 cup finely chopped celery
1/4 cup finely chopped green bell pepper
2 tablespoons minced onion

1 teaspoon dried mustard
1 tablespoon lemon juice
1/3 cup light mayonnaise or salad
  dressing*
1 9-inch deep-dish, frozen pie shell*

HAM AND SWISS PASTRY BAKE

Combine ham, cheese, celery, bell pepper, onion, mustard and lemon juice in a 1-gallon plastic bag, and store in freezer.

To prepare for serving, thaw ham mixture, add mayonnaise, and put into a 9-inch pie shell. Bake uncovered in a preheated 375° oven for 25 to 35 minutes till golden brown. Serve hot. **Makes 6 servings.**

Summary of processes: Cut 2 cups ham into cubes; grate 1 cup Swiss cheese; chop 1/4 cup celery and 1/4 cup bell pepper

Freeze in: 1-gallon bag

Serve with: Frozen Fruit Medley (page 143)

STOVE-TOP BARBECUED CHICKEN

1 teaspoon vegetable oil
1 cup finely chopped onion
1/3 cup catsup
1/3 cup water
4 teaspoons white vinegar
4 teaspoons brown sugar

1 1/2 teaspoons Worcestershire sauce
1/2 teaspoon chili powder
1/4 teaspoon crushed celery seeds
2 pounds skinless chicken pieces
1 8-ounce package spinach or wide egg noodles*

Heat oil in a large, nonstick skillet; sauté onion until tender. Stir in catsup, water, vinegar, brown sugar, Worcestershire sauce, chili powder and celery seeds. Bring sauce to a boil. Add the chicken to the skillet, placing the side down that has the skin removed; spoon sauce over the pieces. Bring to a boil; reduce heat. Cover and simmer 30 minutes. Turn chicken pieces, and simmer covered for about 20 minutes more or until chicken is cooked through. Cool and freeze chicken and sauce.

To prepare for serving, thaw chicken and sauce; put in a large skillet, and cook over medium heat, stirring constantly until bubbly. Cook package of spinach or egg noodles according to package directions; serve chicken over noodles. **Makes 4 servings.**

Summary of processes: Chop 1 cup onion

Freeze in: 4-cup container

Serve with: Corn on the cob, **Low-Calorie Chocolate Cake** (page 140)

2 cups cooked, chopped chicken
1 3-ounce package cream cheese, softened
1 tablespoon chopped chives
2 tablespoons milk

Salt to taste
1/2 cup crushed, seasoned crouton crumbs*
2 packages refrigerated crescent rolls*
1/4 cup melted margarine*

Mix chicken, cream cheese, chives, milk and salt in a medium bowl (mixing with hands works best) to make filling, and store in a 1-quart freezer bag. Put crouton crumbs in another 1-quart bag, attach it to bag of chicken filling, and freeze them. Refrigerate crescent rolls.

To prepare for serving, thaw chicken mixture. Unroll crescent rolls. Each tube will contain 4 rectangles of dough with a diagonal perforation. Press dough along each perforation so that the rectangle halves will not separate. Place about 1/4 cup of chicken mixture into the center of each rectangle. Fold dough over the filling, and pinch the edges to seal tightly. Dip each packet in melted margarine, and coat with crouton crumbs. Place packets on a baking sheet. Bake in a preheated 350° oven for 20 minutes or until golden brown. Packets are good either hot or cold. (Serve early in the month before date expires on crescent rolls.) **Makes 8 packets.**

Summary of processes: Chop 2 cups cooked chicken and 1 tablespoon chives

Freeze in: 2 1-quart bags

Serve with: Smoky Corn Chowder (page 144), baked apples stuffed with plump raisins

Note: These packets are a favorite with children.

WILD RICE CHICKEN

1 6¼-ounce package quick-cooking, long grain and wild rice
1 cup cooked, chopped chicken
1 8-ounce can sliced water chestnuts, drained

1 cup finely chopped celery
1¼ cups finely chopped onion
1 cup light mayonnaise*
1 10¾-ounce can condensed cream of mushroom soup*

Cook rice according to package directions. Combine rice with chopped chicken, water chestnuts, celery and onion; put mixture in a 1-gallon freezer bag.

To prepare for serving, thaw rice and chicken mixture, remove from bag, and place in a 2½ quart baking dish. Stir mayonnaise and condensed cream of mushroom soup together, and spread over top of chicken. Bake covered in a preheated 325° oven for 1 hour. **Makes 6 servings.**

Summary of processes: Chop 1 cup cooked chicken, 1 cup celery and 1¼ cups onion

Freeze in: 1-gallon bag

Serve with: Cooked green beans, peach halves with cottage cheese topped with a maraschino cherry, and **Portuguese Sweet Bread** (page 134)

FRUITY CURRIED CHICKEN

¾ cup regular, uncooked rice
1 cup finely chopped onion
2½ cups chicken broth
1 8¾-ounce can apricots, drained
2¼ cups cooked, diced chicken

¾ teaspoon salt
¼ teaspoon curry powder
¼ teaspoon pepper
2 teaspoons lemon juice
⅓ cup raisins

In a medium saucepan, heat rice, onion and chicken broth to a boil, stirring once or twice. Reduce heat to low; cover and simmer 15 minutes. Do not lift lid or stir rice. Drain and cut apricots into pieces. Combine all ingredients. Allow to cool, and store in freezer.

To prepare for serving, thaw entrée, put in baking dish and cover with foil. Bake in a preheated 350° degree oven for 1 hour. (Add a small amount of liquid if it becomes too dry after baking.) **Makes 4 servings.**

Summary of processes: Chop 1 cup onion and 2¼ cups cooked chicken

Freeze in: 4-cup container

Serve with: Fresh Baked Asparagus (page 145)

1 10-ounce package frozen, chopped
   spinach
1/2 cup sliced green onions
2 tablespoons margarine
2 tablespoons all-purpose flour
1 cup milk

1 cup soda cracker crumbs
1 cup grated Parmesan cheese
8 boneless chicken breast halves,
   skinned, about 3 3/4 pounds
1 cup cooked, cubed ham

HEAVENLY CHICKEN

In a small saucepan, cook spinach according to package directions; drain well. In a medium saucepan, make white sauce; sauté onions in margarine over low heat until tender. Stir in flour, adding milk all at once. Cook over low heat, stirring constantly until bubbly. Boil and stir 1 minute more until smooth and thickened.

Combine cracker crumbs and cheese. Dip chicken breast halves in crumb mixture to coat lightly. Arrange breast halves in a 13x9x2-inch baking dish. Seal leftover crumb mixture in a 1-quart bag.

Stir spinach and ham into white sauce; spoon sauce over chicken breasts. Allow to cool and cover baking dish with foil, attaching bag of crumb mixture to side of dish.

To prepare for serving, thaw dish, and bake covered in a preheated 350° oven for 60 to 75 minutes. Uncover, and sprinkle top with crumbs. Bake 10 minutes more. **Makes 8 servings**.

Summary of processes: Slice 1/2 cup green onions; crush 1 cup cracker crumbs; cut 1 cup ham into cubes

Freeze in: 13x9x2-inch baking dish; 1-quart bag

Serve with: Pineapple chunks and mandarin oranges sprinkled with shredded coconut, **Cranberry Tea** (page 139)

Note: This is practically a meal in one dish.

CHINESE CHICKEN MORSELS

1 pound boneless, skinless chicken breasts (2 cups)
1/2 cup lemon juice
1/4 cup soy sauce

1/4 cup Dijon mustard
2 teaspoons vegetable oil
1/4 teaspoon cayenne pepper
1 cup regular, uncooked rice*

Cut chicken breasts (kitchen scissors work best) into 1-inch cubes. Mix lemon juice, soy sauce, mustard, oil and pepper. Put marinade and chicken cubes in a 1-gallon bag, and store in the freezer.

To prepare for serving, thaw chicken and remove from marinade. Warm marinade in a small saucepan. Place cubes about an inch apart on broiler pan treated with nonstick spray. Broil 4 to 5 inches from heat for 7 minutes, brushing with marinade once. Turn chicken cubes, and broil another 4 minutes. Meanwhile, prepare rice according to package directions. Heat remaining marinade and serve over rice. **Makes 4 to 5 servings.**

Summary of processes: Cut chicken into 1-inch cubes

Freeze in: 1-gallon bag

Serve with: Sliced, fresh tomatoes or tossed salad, **Spicy Pumpkin Muffins** (page 137)

Note: For a luncheon alternative, toss sautéed or broiled chicken morsels with mixed salad greens, shredded carrots, cherry tomatoes, chopped, green bell pepper, sliced water chestnuts and croutons. Use your favorite low-calorie dressing.

1 12-ounce package seasoned bread
   stuffing (6 cups)
2 tablespoons melted margarine
2 cups chicken broth
3 cups cooked, chopped chicken
1/2 cup finely chopped onion
1/4 cup minced chives
1/2 cup finely chopped celery

1/2 cup light mayonnaise
3/4 teaspoon salt
2 eggs
1 1/2 cups milk
1 10 3/4-ounce can condensed cream of
   mushroom soup
1/2 cup grated mild cheddar cheese

POULET DE FRANCE

In a medium bowl, mix stuffing, melted margarine and 1 1/4 cups broth. Mix chicken, 3/4 cup broth, onions, chives, celery, mayonnaise and salt in another bowl.

Spread half the stuffing in a 13x9x2-inch baking dish treated with nonstick spray. Spread chicken mixture over stuffing. Cover with remaining stuffing. Whisk eggs, milk and soup in a large bowl. Pour sauce evenly over stuffing. Cover dish with foil and freeze. Put cheese in a small freezer bag, and attach it to dish.

To prepare for serving, thaw grated cheese and chicken dish. Bake covered in a preheated 325° oven for 30 minutes. Remove foil, sprinkle with cheese, and continue to bake uncovered for 10 minutes more. **Makes 8 servings.**

Summary of processes: Chop 3 cups cooked chicken, 1/2 cup onions and 1/2 cup celery; mince 1/4 cup chives; grate 1/2 cup mild cheddar cheese

Freeze in: 13x9x2-inch baking dish; 1-quart bag

Serve with: Cooked frozen peas, **Cranberry Tea** (page 139)

Note: This is a super dish to take to a potluck dinner.

MEAL-IN-ONE POTATOES

½ pound freshly ground turkey
½ cup finely chopped onion
1 teaspoon minced garlic (1 clove)
1 cup canned, red kidney beans, drained
1 8-ounce can tomato sauce

½ cup chili sauce
1 teaspoon dried oregano leaves
¼ teaspoon salt
4 medium baking potatoes*

In a medium skillet, cook ground turkey, onion and garlic until turkey is browned; add remaining ingredients except potatoes. Bring to a boil; reduce heat. Simmer 5 minutes. Cool and freeze in a 1-quart bag.

To serve, thaw filling. Prepare and bake potatoes in a preheated 400° oven for 1 hour or until done. Heat filling until bubbly. Split tops of baked potatoes lengthwise, and fluff pulp with a fork. Top each potato with filling. **Makes 4 servings.**

Summary of processes: Chop ½ cup onion, mince 1 clove garlic

Freeze in: 1-quart bag

Serve with: Smoky Corn Chowder (page 144)

TERIYAKI CHICKEN

½ cup soy sauce
½ cup sugar
1 ½ tablespoons red wine vinegar
2 teaspoons vegetable oil or sesame seed oil

1 small minced garlic clove
¾ teaspoon ground ginger
1 pound boneless, skinless chicken breasts
1 cup regular, uncooked rice*

Mix soy sauce, sugar, vinegar, oil, garlic and ginger to make marinade (reserve 2 tablespoons in a small bowl for **Teriyaki Burgers).** Freeze chicken in marinade in a 1-gallon bag.

When preparing to serve, thaw chicken. Pour chicken and marinade into a baking dish. Bake in a preheated 350° oven for 35 minutes. Prepare rice according to package directions. Serve chicken over rice. **Makes 4 servings.**

Freeze in: 1-gallon bag

Serve with: Cooked French-cut green beans

1 small onion
2 or 3 whole cloves
1 cup cooked, diced chicken
2 quarts chicken broth
1/2 teaspoon salt

1 tablespoon chopped fresh parsley
3 shredded carrots
1/2 cup sliced celery with leaves
1 8-ounce package (use half) tortellini*

MIMI'S CHICKEN SOUP

Peel and cut ends off onion; insert whole cloves into the onion. In a large pot, combine onion, chicken, broth, salt, parsley, carrots and celery. Bring to a boil; reduce heat. Simmer uncovered for 1 1/2 hours. Remove onion. Cool soup, put in container, and store in freezer.

To prepare for serving, thaw soup, put in large pot, and heat until bubbly. Add half a package tortellini, and boil 25 minutes more. **Makes 4 servings.**

Summary of processes: Chop cooked chicken; shred 3 carrots; slice 1/2 cup celery; chop 1 tablespoon parsley

Freeze in: 8-cup container

Serve with: Swedish Rye Bread (page 136)

BAKED HERB FISH FILLETS

4 fish fillets (about 1 1/4 pounds orange roughy or sole)*
1/2 cup Italian-flavored bread crumbs
1/4 cup grated Parmesan cheese
1/4 teaspoon garlic powder

1/4 teaspoon salt
1 egg white, lightly beaten*
4 to 5 new potatoes*
1 small lemon*

Freeze fish fillets in a 1-gallon bag. Combine bread crumbs, Parmesan cheese, garlic powder and salt in a 1-quart bag; attach to fish fillet package.

To prepare to serve, thaw fish and herbs. Lightly beat egg white, and dip fillets in it. Put fillets one at a time in bag with herb mixture; make sure each is coated. Remove and arrange fillets in baking dish. Bake in preheated 375° oven for about 15 minutes (until fish flakes easily) or in microwave oven on high for 4 to 5 minutes.

At the same time, prepare new potatoes. Peel a strip around the center of each potato. Heat 1 cup salted water to a boil; add potatoes. Cover, heat till boiling; reduce heat. Simmer tightly covered until tender, 30 to 35 minutes; drain. Serve potatoes with fish and lemon wedges. **Makes 4 servings.**

Freeze in: 1-gallon and 1-quart bag

Serve with: Cooked zucchini, **Mimi's Nutritious Bread** (page 133)

AZTEC QUICHE

1 1/4 cups grated Monterey Jack cheese
3/4 cup grated mild cheddar cheese
1 9-inch deep-dish frozen pie shell
1 4-ounce can diced green chilies

1 cup half-and-half
3 eggs, beaten lightly
1/2 teaspoon salt
1/8 teaspoon ground cumin

Spread Monterey Jack cheese and half of cheddar over bottom of pie shell. Sprinkle diced chilies over cheeses. Stir together in a bowl the half-and-half, eggs and seasonings. Pour carefully into pie shell. Sprinkle with remaining cheddar. Cover pie with foil, and put in freezer.

To prepare for serving, thaw pie and remove foil. Bake uncovered in a preheated 325° oven for 40 to 50 minutes. **Makes 6 to 8 servings.**

Summary of processes: Grate 1 1/4 cups Monterey Jack cheese and 3/4 cup mild cheddar cheese

Freeze in: 9-inch oven-proof quiche or pie pan

Serve with: Fresh fruit salad, **Cinnamon Logs** (page 137)

6 bread slices, cut in cubes
2 cups grated mild cheddar cheese
1 cup cooked, cubed ham
¼ cup finely chopped green bell pepper
½ cup finely chopped onion
6 eggs
3 cups milk

Mix bread, cheese, ham, bell pepper and onion; spread in a 13x9x2-inch baking dish treated with nonstick spray. Whisk eggs and milk, and pour over top. Cover dish with foil, and freeze.

To prepare for serving, thaw dish, and bake uncovered in a preheated 375° oven for 45 minutes. **Makes 8 to 10 servings.**

Summary of processes: Cut bread and ham into cubes; grate 2 cups mild cheddar cheese; chop ¼ cup green bell pepper and ½ cup onion

Freeze in: 13x9x2-inch baking dish

Serve with: Frozen Fruit Medley (page 143)

Note: This dish is good with 6 slices cooked, crumbled bacon instead of ham. You can also make this dish the night before, refrigerate it, and serve it the next morning. It's nice for company brunch after church.

1 pound lean ground beef
2 tablespoons teriyaki sauce (see recipe for Teriyaki Chicken marinade)
4 sandwich rolls*

Mix teriyaki sauce into ground beef; form four patties. Freeze patties in a 1-gallon freezer bag with a piece of waxed paper between each patty. Freeze sandwich rolls.

To serve, thaw rolls and patties. Grill or fry meat to desired pinkness. Serve on warmed sandwich rolls. **Makes 4 servings.**

Freeze in: 1-gallon bag

Serve with: Potato salad, pickles and ripe olives

BARBEQUED FILLETS

4 strips bacon
1 pound lean ground beef
Salt
Lemon pepper
¼ cup grated Parmesan cheese

1 2-ounce can mushroom stems and pieces, drained
1 tablespoon minced onion
2 tablespoons finely chopped green bell pepper

In a small skillet or microwave, cook bacon until limp. Drain bacon on paper towel. Pat ground beef on waxed paper into a 12x8x¼-inch rectangle. Sprinkle lightly with salt and lemon pepper. Top with Parmesan cheese.

Combine mushrooms, onion and bell pepper; sprinkle evenly over ground beef. Roll ground beef like a jelly roll, starting from the longest side. Cut into four, 1½-inch-wide slices. Wrap edge of each slice with a strip of partially cooked bacon, securing with wooden picks. Freeze hamburgers with a piece of waxed paper between each patty.

To serve, thaw patties; grill over medium coals 8 minutes. Turn and grill 8 more minutes or to desired doneness; Or broil hamburgers. **Makes 4 servings.**

Summary of processes: Chop 2 tablespoons green bell pepper

Freeze in: 1-gallon bag

Serve with: Twice-Baked Potatoes Deluxe (page 145), **Marinated Veggies** (page 146)

RAVIOLI SOUP

1 pound lean ground beef (2 ½ cups browned meat)

¼ cup soft bread crumbs

¼ cup grated Parmesan cheese

¾ teaspoon onion salt

2 teaspoons minced garlic (2 cloves)

1 tablespoon olive oil or vegetable oil

1 ½ cups finely chopped onion

1 28-ounce can Italian-style or plain crushed tomatoes in puree

1 6-ounce can tomato paste

1 14 ½-ounce can beef broth or bouillon

1 cup water

½ teaspoon sugar

½ teaspoon dried basil leaves

¼ teaspoon dried thyme leaves

¼ teaspoon dried oregano leaves

¼ cup chopped fresh parsley

1 12-ounce package plain ravioli without sauce* (located in the frozen or refrigerated section)

Grated Parmesan cheese*

Brown the ground beef in a large pot; combine remaining ingredients except frozen ravioli and additional Parmesan cheese. Bring soup to a boil; reduce heat. Cover and simmer 10 minutes, stirring occasionally. Cool, put in container, and freeze.

To prepare for serving, thaw soup base and put in a large pot. Bring to a boil; reduce heat. Simmer uncovered for at least 30 minutes, stirring occasionally. Thaw and cook ravioli according to package directions until just tender. Drain ravioli; add to soup. Salt to taste. Serve with Parmesan cheese. **Makes 6 servings.**

Summary of processes: Mince 2 cloves garlic; chop 1 ¾ cup onion, ¼ cup parsley

Freeze in: 8-cup container

Serve with: Tossed green salad and **Dawn's French Bread** (page 135)

MANICOTTI

1 8-ounce package manicotti
1 tablespoon vegetable oil
1 15-ounce carton part-skim ricotta cheese
1 16-ounce carton low-fat cottage cheese
1 cup grated mozzarella cheese

$^1/_3$ cup grated Parmesan cheese
1 teaspoon salt
$^1/_4$ teaspoon pepper
1 tablespoon chopped fresh parsley
2 eggs
2$^1/_2$ cups Spaghetti Sauce

Boil manicotti according to package directions, adding oil to water so they won't stick together. Meanwhile, mix ricotta cheese, cottage cheese, mozzarella and Parmesan cheeses, salt, pepper, parsley and eggs.

Drain manicotti; run cold water over it. Stuff each manicotti with cheese mixture. Place them in a 3-quart casserole, and pour sauce around stuffed manicotti. Cover dish with foil and freeze.

To prepare for serving, thaw dish. Bake covered in a preheated 350° oven for 45 minutes. Uncover and bake for 15 minutes more. **Makes 8 servings.**

Summary of processes: Grate 1 cup mozzarella cheese; chop 1 tablespoon parsley

Freeze in: 3-quart casserole

Serve with: Spinach salad

1 1/2 pounds lean ground beef (3 3/4 cups browned)

1/3 cup finely chopped onion (1/4 cup sautéed)

1 envelope taco seasoning mix

1 4-ounce can diced green chilies, drained

1 cup milk

1 cup biscuit baking mix

2 eggs

1 cup grated mild cheddar cheese

2 tomatoes, sliced*

1 8-ounce carton sour cream*

1 chopped tomato*

Shredded lettuce (enough to garnish pie)*

In a large skillet, cook and stir ground beef and onion until beef is brown; drain. Combine beef with taco seasoning mix, and spread in a 10-inch pie plate. Sprinkle with chilies. Beat milk, baking mix and eggs until smooth, 15 seconds on high in a blender or 1 minute with hand beater. Pour milk mixture over beef in pie plate. Cover plate with foil, and freeze. Keep 1-quart bag of grated cheese with pie.

To prepare for serving, thaw pie. Bake uncovered in a preheated 400° oven for 35 minutes. Top with sliced tomatoes; sprinkle with cheese. Bake until golden brown, 8 to 10 minutes. Top with sour cream, chopped tomato and shredded lettuce. **Makes 6 to 8 servings.**

Summary of processes: Chop 1/3 cup onion; grate 1 cup cheddar cheese

Freeze in: 10-inch quiche or pie plate; 1-quart bag

Serve with: Guacamole dip with tortilla chips, fruit salad

JOES TO GO

1 pound lean ground beef (3 1/2 cups browned)

3/4 cup finely chopped onion (1/2 cup sautéed)

1 1/2 teaspoons garlic salt

1/8 teaspoon pepper

1/2 cup chili sauce

1/4 cup brown sugar

1 tablespoon white vinegar

1 tablespoon prepared mustard

1 8-ounce can tomato sauce

6 hamburger buns*

In a large skillet, cook and stir ground beef and onion until beef is brown; drain. Add garlic salt, pepper, chili sauce, brown sugar, white vinegar, mustard and tomato sauce. Bring to a boil; reduce heat. Simmer uncovered 10 minutes, stirring occasionally. Cool and freeze. Keep with hamburger buns.

To prepare for serving, thaw hamburger sauce and buns. Heat sauce until bubbly, and serve on warmed buns. **Makes enough for 6 buns.**

Summary of processes: Chop 1 1/2 cups onion

Freeze in: 8-cup container

Serve with: Potato chips and carrot and celery sticks

1 1/2 pounds lean ground beef (3 3/4 cups browned)
1 17-ounce can corn, drained
2 eggs, slightly beaten
1 cup small curd cottage cheese with chives, drained
1 tablespoon all-purpose flour
1 8-ounce can tomato sauce
1/2 teaspoon minced garlic
1/4 teaspoon ground cinnamon
1 cup grated mozzarella cheese*

CHEESY CORN CASSEROLE

In a large skillet, cook and stir ground beef until brown; drain. Meanwhile, spread corn in bottom of an 8x8x2-inch baking dish. Combine eggs and cottage cheese; spread mixture over corn.

Stir flour into browned ground beef; cook 1 minute, stirring constantly. Add tomato sauce, garlic and cinnamon to meat mixture, and stir together. Layer meat mixture on top of cottage cheese and eggs. Cover dish with foil, and put in freezer. Put mozzarella in 1-quart freezer bag; tape to baking dish.

To prepare for serving, thaw meat dish and cheese. Sprinkle cheese on top. Bake uncovered in a preheated 350° oven for 30 minutes. **Makes 6 servings.**

Summary of processes: Mince 1/2 teaspoon garlic; grate 1 cup mozzarella cheese

Freeze in: 8x8x2-inch baking dish; 1-quart bag

Serve with: Beets, **Spicy Pumpkin Muffins** (page 137)

2 3/4-inch-thick, cooked ham slices (from center of ham)*
Prepared mustard*
Brown sugar*
1 cup milk (about)*
4 medium baking potatoes*

HAM DINNER SLICES

Freeze ham slices in 1-gallon bag.

To serve, thaw ham slices. Prepare potatoes and bake in a preheated 400° oven for about 1 hour or until done. Place ham slices in a single layer in the bottom of an 8x8x2-inch baking dish treated with nonstick spray. Spread mustard on top of each slice; sprinkle brown sugar over mustard. Pour enough milk over ham slices to come halfway up their sides. Bake uncovered 45 minutes. **Makes 4 servings.**

Freeze in: 1-gallon bag

Serve with: Cooked green beans, **Orange Spiced Tea** (page 139)

CHAPTER 4

"Abigail lost no time. She took two hundred loaves of bread, two skins of wine, five dressed sheep, five seahs of roasted grain, a hundred cakes of raisins and two hundred cakes of pressed figs, and loaded them on donkeys"

(1 Samuel 25:18, NIV).

MENU CALENDAR

SUN.	MON.	TUES.	WED.	THURS.	FRI.	SAT.
	1 Eat Out Cooking Day!	**2** Split Pea Soup	**3** Salad Bowl Puff	**4** Jack Burgers	**5** Deborah's Sweet and Sour Chicken	**6** French Stew
7 Shish Kebabs	**8** Chicken and Rice Pilaf	**9** Grandma's Chili	**10** Crustless Spinach Quiche	**11** Grilled Ham Slices	**12** Green Chili Enchiladas	**13** Chicken á la King
14 Sausage and Rice	**15** Oriental Chicken	**16** Marinated Flank Steak	**17** Saucy Hot Dogs	**18** Currant Ham Loaf	**19** Lasagna	**20** Oven Barbecued Chicken & Cheesy Biscuits
21 Chicken Broccoli	**22** Balkan Meatballs	**23** Baked Beans and Hamburger	**24** Jan's Sandwiches	**25** Bird's Nest Pie	**26** Chicken Tetrazzini	**27** French Dip
28 Lemon Chicken	**29** Grilled Fish	**30** Mexican Stroganoff				

GROCERY SHOPPING AND STAPLES LISTS

An asterisk (*) after an item indicates that it should be stored until you cook the dish it will be served with. For example, the jar of prepared mustard and the currant jelly will not be needed until the day you serve the entrées that accompany them. Mark those items as a reminder that you will need them for an entrée.

When entrées require perishable foods to be refrigerated until served, you may want to prepare those dishes right away or buy the food the week you plan to make the dish. For example, fresh mushrooms would spoil by the end of a month.

For the month two entrée plan, you will need these food items as well as the ones in the staples list that follows:

Canned Goods

1 bottle barbecue sauce (1 cup, your favorite)*
1 10³/4-ounce can beef consommé
1 8-ounce bottle chili sauce
2 10³/4-ounce cans condensed cream of chicken soup
4 10³/4-ounce cans condensed cream of mushroom soup
1 10-ounce jar currant jelly*
1 4-ounce can diced green chilies
1 4-ounce can green chili salsa
1 16-ounce can whole green beans
1 15-ounce can kidney beans
1 8¹/2-ounce can whole onions (or frozen small onions)
1 16-ounce can small peas
1 24-ounce bottle red wine vinegar (about 2 cups)
1 8-ounce, 3 4-ounce and 1 2-ounce cans mushroom stems and pieces
1 6-ounce jar prepared mustard*

1 2-ounce jar pimientos
1 31-ounce can pork and beans
2 8-ounce cans pineapple chunks (1*)
1 17-ounce bottle soy sauce (about 1¹/8 cups)
3 16-ounce cans peeled tomatoes
1 12-ounce and 2 6-ounce cans tomato paste
1 15-ounce and 2 8-ounce cans tomato sauce
2 8-ounce cans sliced water chestnuts

Grains, Pasta and Rice

1 10-ounce tube Hungry Jack Biscuits*
¹/2 cup fine, dry bread crumbs
6 hot dog buns*
16 sandwich or onion rolls (8*)
4 hamburger buns*
1 8-ounce package lasagna
1 5-ounce can chow mein noodles*
1 12-ounce and 1 8-ounce package wide egg noodles*

12 ounces dry, green split peas
1 32-ounce and 1 16-ounce package
   regular rice
1 16-ounce package spaghetti
8 to 12 flour tortillas
1 6 1/4-ounce package fast-cooking long
   grain and wild rice (use Uncle Ben's
   if available)

Dry Ingredients and Seasonings
1 package onion soup mix
1 package French's or Good Seasons
   French dip or brown gravy mix*

Frozen Foods
1 1/4 pounds frozen fish fillets (halibut,
   swordfish or orange roughy)*
1 10-ounce package chopped broccoli
1 10-ounce package (use half) peas
1 10-ounce package chopped spinach
1 package patty shells*

Dairy Products
3/4 cup margarine or butter
13 eggs (2*)
1 16-ounce carton small curd, low-fat
   cottage cheese
2 12-ounce cartons large curd, low-fat
   cottage cheese
4 8-ounce cartons sour cream (or 1
   carton 8-ounce low-fat yogurt for
one   of the cartons of sour cream)
1 8-ounce jar Cheez Whiz
12 ounces (3 cups) grated mild cheddar
   cheese
22 ounces Monterey Jack cheese (4
thin   slices, 7 cups grated)

16 ounces sliced mozzarella cheese
7 ounces (about 1 3/4 cups) grated
   Parmesan cheese
1 cup half-and-half
1 quart milk

Meat and Poultry
2 pounds boneless, cubed, top sirloin
   steak
7 1/4 pounds lean ground beef (or
   turkey)
1/2 pound ground pork
1 1/3 pounds flank steak
2 pounds round steak
3 to 4 pounds sirloin tip or boneless
   beef rump roast*
3 pounds beef stew meat
12 1/2 pounds whole chickens or 10
   pounds chicken breasts
4 boneless, skinless chicken breasts
3 1/2 pounds chicken pieces (breasts,
   thighs or drumsticks)
4 strips bacon
5 1/2 pounds cooked ham (2 pounds
   ground, 1 1/2 pounds cubed, and
2 pounds from the center portion cut
   in 2 3/4-inch-thick dinner slices*)
1 1/2 pounds ground turkey
2 pounds bulk Italian or turkey sausage
6 hot dogs or turkey franks*
1 2 1/2-ounce package thin-sliced,
   corned beef luncheon meat

Produce
4 carrots
1 bunch celery

7 cloves garlic (7 teaspoons minced)
1 bunch green onions
5 green bell peppers (4 1/4 cups chopped, 1/2*)

4 ounces whole fresh mushrooms*
4 1/4 pounds yellow onions
5 to 6 new potatoes
Half a pint box cherry tomatoes*

STAPLES LIST

Make sure you have the following staples on hand; add those you don't have to the above shopping list:

ground allspice
dried basil leaves
bay leaves
biscuit baking mix (^{1}/2 cup)
brown sugar (1 ^{1}/8 cups)
catsup (^{1}/4 cup)
chicken bouillon cube
chili powder
ground cinnamon
cornstarch
seasoned croutons (^{1}/3 cup crushed)
curry powder
all-purpose flour (about ^{3}/4 cup)
garlic powder
ground ginger
lemon juice (^{1}/3 cup)

light mayonnaise (about 1 cup)
minced onion
minute tapioca (^{1}/4 cup)
nonstick spray
ground nutmeg
olive oil
onion powder
onion salt
paprika
parsley flakes
pepper
salt
seasoned salt
soda crackers (1 cup crumbs)
sugar (^{1}/2 cup plus ^{3}/4 teaspoon)
dried thyme leaves
vegetable oil (about ^{3}/4 cup)
white vinegar (^{1}/2 cup)
Worcestershire sauce

The following list of freezer containers or baking dishes will be needed for the entrées. These are not the only containers you could use, but this list gives you an idea of the size and number of containers you'll need.

Heavy aluminum foil:
Jan's Sandwiches

5 1-quart freezer bags:
Green Chili Enchiladas, Bird's Nest Pie, Grilled Fish, Crustless Spinach Quiche, Oven Barbecued Chicken and Cheesy Biscuits

11 1-gallon freezer bags:
Grilled Ham Slices, Balkan Meatballs, Jack Burgers, Sausage and Rice, Lemon Chicken, Chicken à la King, Oriental Chicken, Salad Bowl Puff, Currant Ham Loaf, Marinated Flank Steak, Oven Barbecued Chicken and Cheesy Biscuits

1 2-cup container:
Grandma's Chili for **Saucy Hot Dogs**

1 5-cup container: **Baked Beans and Hamburger**

6 6-cup containers:
Split Pea Soup, Grandma's Chili, Chicken Tetrazzini (2), Shish Kebabs, Mexican Stroganoff

1 8-cup container:
Deborah's Sweet and Sour Chicken

1 14-cup container:
French Stew

1 11x7x1 1/2-inch baking dish:
Chicken and Rice Pilaf

3 13x9x2-inch baking dishes:
Lasagna, Green Chili Enchiladas, Chicken Broccoli

2 10-inch quiche or pie plates:
Bird's Nest Pie, Crustless Spinach Quiche

FREEZER CONTAINERS

THE DAY BEFORE COOKING DAY

1. Freeze hamburger buns, hot dog buns, patty shells, frozen fish fillets, ham dinner slices, sirloin tip or beef rump roast, and all but 8 of the sandwich rolls.

2. Refrigerate 1/2 green bell pepper, whole fresh mushrooms, 1 whole onion and cherry tomatoes for **Shish Kebabs**.

3. Refrigerate 7 1/2 pounds lean ground beef, 4 boneless chicken breasts and 1 pound chicken pieces. Freeze remaining 2 1/2 pounds chicken pieces for **Oven Barbecued Chicken and Cheesy Biscuits** in a 1-gallon bag marked with name of recipe.

4. Cover remaining whole chickens or breasts with at least 9 cups water in a large pot. Bring to a boil; reduce heat. Cover and simmer until thickest pieces are done, about 45 minutes to 1 hour. Cool chicken until ready to handle. Remove meat from bones and skin. Cut chicken into bite-size pieces with kitchen scissors, which are easier to use than a knife. Refrigerate chicken pieces in two plastic bags. (You will need 15 1/2 cups diced, cooked chicken.)

5. Refrigerate 3 cups chicken broth; discard remaining broth or use for soup.

6. Set out appliances, bowls, canned goods, dry ingredients, freezer containers and recipes.

7. Rinse split peas, and soak them covered with cold water overnight.

8. Start **French Stew** in crockpot (just before bed).

Make sure you've cleared the table and counters of unnecessary kitchenware to allow plenty of working room. It also helps to have fresh, damp washcloths and towels for wiping your hands and the cooking area. The day will go a lot smoother if you keep cleaning and organizing as you work.

Before you prepare a recipe, gather all the spices and ingredients in the assembly area to save time and steps. When you finish the recipe, remove unneeded items, and wipe off the work space.

Before Assembling Dishes:

1. Cool and freeze **French Stew**. Wash out crockpot.

2. Perform all chopping, crushing, grating and slicing tasks.
Bacon: Dice 1/4 pound and 3 strips (put in separate dishes).
Ham: Dice 2 cups (if the butcher didn't do this).
Round steak: Cut into bite-size pieces.
Onions: Chop 11 2/3 cups fine; chop 1 3/4 cups coarsely for **Shish Kebabs** and **Deborah's Sweet and Sour Chicken**.
Green onions: Chop onion bulbs only; discard green tops.
Green bell peppers: Chop 3 1/4 cups; cut 1 cup in coarse pieces for **Deborah's Sweet and Sour Chicken**; save half of pepper for **Shish Kebabs**.
Celery: Chop 1 1/3 cups fine and 1 cup in coarse pieces; put in separate containers.
Carrots: Peel and slice 3/4 cup and 3 large; put in separate containers.

Garlic: Mince 7 cloves (7 teaspoons).
Mozzarella cheese: Slice all.
Mild cheddar cheese: Grate all.
Monterey Jack cheese: Cut 4 thin slices; grate remaining cheese.
Crumbs: Crush 1/2 cup fine, dry bread crumbs; 1 cup cracker crumbs; 1/4 cup crouton crumbs.

3. Put 1/2 cup grated mild cheddar cheese in a 1-quart freezer bag; tape it to bag of chicken pieces for **Oven Barbecued Chicken and Cheesy Biscuits**.

4. Cook and stir 5 1/4 pounds ground beef in a large skillet until brown.

5. In another large skillet, sauté 8 1/2 cups onions in margarine until tender.

6. Spray pans or baking dishes you will need with nonstick spray (check list of freezer containers on page 79).

7. Skim and discard fat from chicken broth.

8. Drain browned ground beef and sautéed onions; set them aside.

Assemble Beef Dishes

1. Assemble **Grandma's Chili** in crockpot using 5 cups browned ground beef and 3/4 cup sautéed onions.

2. Start baking sirloin tip or boneless beef rump roast for **French Dip**.

3. Make **Lasagna** using 2 1/2 cups browned ground beef.

4. Start **Mexican Stroganoff** simmering in a large saucepan.

5. Assemble **Baked Beans and Hamburger** using 2 cups browned ground beef and 1/2 cup sautéed onions.

6. Prepare **Balkan Meatballs**.

7. While meatballs are broiling, assemble **Green Chili Enchiladas** using 3 3/4 cups browned ground beef and 3/4 cup sautéed onions.

8. Make **Jack Burgers**.

9. Freeze beef dishes.

Assemble Sausage Dishes

1. Brown 2 pounds of Italian or turkey sausage; drain.

2. Break 1-pound package spaghetti in half, and cook as directed on package until al dente; drain. Toss half the noodles in 1/2 tablespoon oil to prevent noodles from sticking together; set aside for **Chicken Tetrazzini**.

3. Assemble **Bird's Nest Pie**, using remaining half of noodles.

4. Prepare **Sausage and Rice**.

5. Freeze sausage dishes.

Assemble Chicken Dishes

1. Complete **Chicken Tetrazzini**.

2. Prepare **Deborah's Sweet and Sour Chicken**.

3. Make **Lemon Chicken.**

4. Complete **Chicken à la King**.

5. Assemble **Chicken Broccoli**.

6. Prepare **Chicken and Rice Pilaf**.

7. Make **Oriental Chicken**.

8. Freeze chicken dishes.

Assemble Ham Dishes

1. Start **Split Pea Soup** simmering.

2. Assemble **Salad Bowl Puff**.

3. Complete **Currant Ham Loaf**.

4. Freeze ham dishes.

Assemble Miscellaneous Dishes

1. Assemble marinade for **Grilled Fish.**

2. Complete **Marinated Flank Steak.**

3. Prepare **Shish Kebabs**.

4. Complete **Crustless Spinach Quiche.**

5. Make **Jan's Sandwiches**.

6. Cool and freeze **Grandma's Chili** and **Split Pea Soup**.

7. Cool and slice sirloin tip or boneless beef rump roast for **French Dip**.

8. Freeze miscellaneous dishes.

RECIPES FOR THE MONTH TWO ENTRÉE PLAN

Each recipe offers complete instructions on how to prepare the dish. Food items with an asterisk (*) won't be prepared until you serve the entrée. For recipes calling for oven baking, preheat oven for about 10 minutes.

"Summary of processes" gives a quick overview of foods that need to be chopped, diced, grated or sliced. "Freeze in" tells what bags and containers will be needed to freeze each entrée. "Serve with" offers suggestions of foods to accompany the meal. Some of the recipes for those foods are included in chapter 6; page numbers are indicated for easy reference. "Note" includes special instructions on how the entrée can be used in other ways.

FRENCH STEW

3 pounds beef stew meat

1 10³/₄-ounce can beef consommé

3 large peeled and sliced carrots

1 16-ounce can whole green beans, drained

1 8¹/₂-ounce can whole onions, drained

1 16-ounce can small peas, drained

1 16-ounce can peeled tomatoes

1 cup water

¹/₃ cup red wine vinegar

¹/₄ cup minute tapioca

1 tablespoon brown sugar

¹/₂ cup fine, dry bread crumbs

1 bay leaf

1 tablespoon salt

¹/₄ teaspoon pepper

Mix ingredients in a large, covered pot. Bake in 250° degree oven for 6 to 8 hours or in a large crockpot 8 to 10 hours on low. Allow to cool, and put in freezer container.

To prepare for serving, thaw stew and heat until bubbly in a large pot. **Makes 8 servings.**

Summary of processes: Peel and slice 3 large carrots

Freeze in: 14-cup container

Serve with: Frozen Fruit Medley (page 143) and **Dawn's French Bread** (page 135)

Note: This stew can be served over cooked wild rice. If you prefer potatoes, cook them and then add to stew when you serve it. (Note that potatoes don't freeze well.) You could also serve this stew on cooking day, freezing what's left over to serve later.

GRANDMA'S CHILI

2 pounds lean ground beef (5 cups browned)
1 1/2 cups finely chopped onion (3/4 cup sautéed)
1 cup chopped green bell pepper
1 tablespoon Worcestershire sauce
3/4 teaspoon chili powder
1/4 teaspoon ground cinnamon
1/8 teaspoon garlic powder
Salt and black pepper to taste
1 15-ounce can kidney beans, drained
1 16-ounce can peeled tomatoes
1 6-ounce can tomato paste
1 15-ounce can tomato sauce

Brown ground beef with onions in a large saucepan; add remaining ingredients. Bring to a boil; reduce heat. Cover and simmer over low heat for 2 hours on a back burner or in a crockpot on low for 6 hours, stirring occasionally. Cool, freeze in 1 6-cup container and 1 2-cup container for **Saucy Hot Dogs**.

To serve chili, thaw and heat in saucepan until hot and bubbly. **Makes 12 servings.**

Summary of Processes: Chop 1 1/2 cups onion, 1 cup green bell pepper

Freeze in: 6-cup container, **Grandma's Chili**; 2-cup container, **Saucy Hot Dogs**

Serve with: Cornbread, cottage cheese with pineapple chunks and mandarin orange slices

Note: This is a nice warm-up meal on a chilly day.

FRENCH DIP

3 to 4 pounds sirloin tip or boneless beef rump roast
Worcestershire sauce

8 sandwich rolls*
1 packet French's or Good Seasons French dip or brown gravy mix*

Place roast in roasting pan on a piece of heavy aluminum foil large enough to wrap meat in. Douse roast with Worcestershire sauce; seal meat in foil. Bake in preheated oven at 350° for 4 to 5 hours on middle rack.

Remove roast from oven; allow it to sit twenty minutes before slicing. Save meat juices and put in a 1-gallon bag with sliced meat.

To serve, thaw sandwich rolls and roast and juices. Pour juices into a saucepan; add seasoning packet. Bring to a boil, reduce heat, and simmer according to package directions. Warm sandwich rolls and meat in a small amount of juice. Serve thin slices of roast in sandwich rolls with bowls of juice for dipping. **Makes 6 to 8 servings.**

Freeze in: 1-gallon bag

Serve with: Waldorf salad, carrot strips

1 pound lean ground beef (2 1/2 cups browned)
1 teaspoon minced garlic (1 clove)
1 tablespoon parsley flakes
1 tablespoon dried basil leaves
1 1/2 teaspoons salt
1 16-ounce can peeled tomatoes
1 12-ounce can tomato paste

1 8-ounce package lasagna
2 12-ounce cartons large curd, low-fat cottage cheese
2 eggs, beaten
1/2 teaspoon pepper
2 tablespoons parsley flakes
1/2 cup grated Parmesan cheese
12 ounces sliced mozzarella cheese

LASAGNA

In a large saucepan, mix browned ground beef, garlic, parsley, basil, salt, tomatoes and tomato paste. Bring to a boil; reduce heat. Simmer uncovered for 30 minutes, stirring frequently.

Cook noodles according to package directions until al dente (firm to the bite); drain. Combine cottage cheese, eggs, pepper, parsley flakes and Parmesan cheese. Grease a 13x9x2-inch baking dish. Place a layer of noodles in dish, spread half the cottage cheese mixture over noodles, layer with half the mozzarella, top with half the sauce mixture. Repeat process, topping with noodles and covering with sauce. Wrap dish with foil and freeze.

To prepare for serving, thaw lasagna. Bake uncovered in pre-heated 375° degree oven for 30 to 40 minutes. **Makes 8 servings.**

Summary of processes: Mince 1 clove garlic; slice 12 ounces mozzarella cheese

Freeze in: 13x9x2-inch baking dish

Serve with: Tossed green salad

Note: Invite youth group members or harried youth group workers over for **Lasagna**.

MEXICAN STROGANOFF

2 pounds round steak
1 cup finely chopped onion
2 teaspoons minced garlic (2 cloves)
2 tablespoons vegetable oil
1/3 cup red wine vinegar
1 3/4 cups water
1/2 cup chili sauce
1 tablespoon paprika
1 tablespoon chili powder

2 teaspoons seasoned salt
1 teaspoon soy sauce
1 8-ounce can mushroom stems and
  pieces, drained
1 8-ounce carton (1 cup) sour cream or
  low-fat yogurt*
3 tablespoons all-purpose flour*
1 12-ounce package wide egg noodles*

Cut steak into bite-size pieces. Cook and stir steak, onion and garlic in oil in a large saucepan over medium heat until brown. Drain off oil. Stir vinegar, water, chili sauce, paprika, chili powder, seasoned salt, soy sauce and mushrooms into steak mixture. Bring to a boil; reduce heat. Cover and simmer 1 hour until meat is tender. Cool and store in freezer container.

To prepare for serving, thaw meat mixture and heat in saucepan until bubbly. Cook egg noodles according to package directions. Stir sour cream or low-fat yogurt and flour together; combine with stroganoff. Heat to a boil, stirring constantly. Reduce heat; simmer and stir about 1 minute. Serve stroganoff over noodles. **Makes 6 to 8 servings.**

Summary of processes: Cut steak in bite-size pieces; chop 1 cup onion; mince 2 cloves garlic

Freeze in: 6-cup container

Serve with: Tomatoes stuffed with guacamole, corn on the cob

3 strips bacon, diced

3/4 pound lean ground beef (2 cups browned)

1 1/4 cups finely chopped onions (or 1/2 cup sautéed)

1 31-ounce can pork and beans in tomato sauce

1 8-ounce can tomato sauce

1/4 cup brown sugar

1/4 cup catsup

Salt and pepper to taste

Brown bacon; drain on a paper towel. In a large skillet, brown ground beef and sauté onions until tender. Mix in bacon and remaining ingredients, put in container, and freeze.

To prepare for serving, thaw beans and hamburger. Bake uncovered in a large baking dish in preheated 350° oven for 30 to 45 minutes. **Makes 6 servings**.

Summary of processes: Dice 1/4 pound bacon; chop 1 1/4 cups onions

Freeze in: 5-cup container

Serve with: Swedish Rye Bread (page 136), corn on the cob, tossed green salad

BALKAN MEATBALLS

1 egg
1/4 cup milk
1/3 cup crushed seasoned croutons
3/4 teaspoon salt
3/4 teaspoon sugar
1/4 teaspoon ground ginger
1/4 teaspoon ground nutmeg
1/4 teaspoon ground allspice

1 pound lean ground beef
1/2 pound ground turkey
2/3 cup finely chopped onion
1 8-ounce package wide egg noodles*
2 tablespoons margarine*
1/4 cup all-purpose flour*
2 cups milk*
Parsley for garnish*

In a medium-size mixing bowl, beat egg with milk. Mix in crushed croutons, salt, sugar and spices. Add beef, turkey and onion; mix thoroughly. Shape meat mixture into meatballs the size of walnuts. Place meatballs on a rimmed cookie sheet; broil until lightly browned. Cool; put meatballs in a large bag, and freeze them.

To prepare for serving, thaw meatballs. Cook noodles according to package directions. At the same time, make white sauce in a large skillet. Melt margarine over low heat. Add flour, stirring constantly until mixture is smooth and bubbly. Gradually stir in milk. Heat to a boil over medium heat, stirring constantly. Boil and stir 1 minute until thick and smooth. Add meatballs to sauce. Bring to a boil; reduce heat. Cover pan; simmer 15 minutes, stirring occasionally. Serve meatballs and sauce over wide egg noodles. Chop parsley; sprinkle over top. **Makes 4 servings.**

Summary of processes: Chop 2/3 cup onion

Freeze in: 1-gallon bag

Serve with: Cooked green beans, **Mimi's Nutritious Bread** (page 133)

1 1/2 pounds lean ground beef (3 3/4 cups browned meat)
1 1/4 cups finely chopped onion (3/4 cup sautéed)
1 tablespoon chili powder
Salt and pepper to taste
8 to 12 flour tortillas

3 cups grated Monterey Jack cheese (1 cup*)
1 10 3/4-ounce can condensed cream of chicken soup
1 1/2 cups sour cream
1 4-ounce can diced, green chilies

GREEN CHILI ENCHILADAS

Brown ground beef, and sauté onions. Combine with chili powder, salt and pepper. Reserve 1 cup cheese in a 1-quart freezer bag to use when serving. Spoon enough meat mixture and cheese on each tortilla to cover a third of it. Roll tortilla beginning at the filled edge. Place seam side down in a 13x9x2-inch baking dish treated with nonstick spray. When tortillas are completed, combine soup, sour cream and green chilies to make a sauce; pour over tortillas. Cover dish with foil, and freeze with bag of cheese taped to it.

To prepare for serving, thaw enchiladas and cheese. Bake uncovered in a preheated 375° oven for 20 to 25 minutes. The last 10 minutes sprinkle cheese on top. **Makes 8 serv-ings.**

Summary of processes: Chop 1 1/4 cups onion; grate 3 cups Monterey Jack cheese

Freeze in: 1-quart bag; 13x9x2-inch baking dish

Serve with: Spanish rice, **Salsa De Lentejas** (page 144)

1 pound lean ground beef
1/2 teaspoon onion salt
1/4 teaspoon freshly ground black pepper

4 thin slices Monterey Jack cheese
4 hamburger buns*

JACK BURGERS

Form ground beef into 8 thin patties. Sprinkle onion salt and black pepper over them. Place a slice of cheese on four of the patties. Cover each with another patty, pinching to seal cheese inside. Freeze in a 1-gallon freezer bag with waxed paper between each set of patties.

To serve, thaw patties and buns. Grill or fry to desired doneness. **Makes 4 servings.**

Summary of processes: Cut 4 slices Monterey Jack cheese

Freeze in: 1-gallon bag

Serve with: Pasta salad, root beer floats

BIRD'S NEST PIE

1 16-ounce package spaghetti (use half)
2 eggs, beaten
1/3 cup grated Parmesan cheese
1/2 cup finely chopped onion (1/4 cup sautéed)
2 tablespoons margarine or butter

1 8-ounce carton sour cream (1 cup)
1 pound bulk Italian or turkey sausage (2 1/2 cups browned)
1 6-ounce can tomato paste
1 cup water
4 ounces sliced mozzarella cheese

Break spaghetti in half, and cook as directed on package until al dente; drain. While spaghetti is warm, combine with eggs and Parmesan cheese. Press spaghetti into bottom and up sides of a well-greased, 10-inch pie plate with a spoon. Sauté onion in margarine, mix with sour cream, and spread over crust.

At the same time, brown sausage in a large skillet; drain fat. Stir in tomato paste and water. Bring to a boil; reduce heat. Simmer uncovered 10 minutes, stirring occasionally. Spoon over sour cream mixture. Cover dish with foil, and freeze. Put cheese slices in a 1-quart bag; attach to side of dish.

To prepare for serving, thaw pie and cheese. Bake pie uncovered in a preheated 350° oven for 25 minutes. Arrange mozzarella slices on top; return pie to oven until cheese melts. **Makes 8 servings.**

Summary of processes: Chop 1/2 cup onion; slice 4 ounces mozzarella cheese

Freeze in: 10-inch quiche or pie plate; 1-quart bag

Serve with: Strawberry gelatin, cooked fresh broccoli

Note: If you double this recipe, use 3 9-inch pie plates.

1 6 1/4-ounce box fast-cooking long grain
   and wild rice
1 pound bulk Italian or turkey sausage
1 1/4 cups finely chopped onion (1 cup
   sautéed)
1 8-ounce can sliced water chestnuts,
   drained

1 cup chopped, green bell pepper
1 cup chopped celery
1 4-ounce can mushrooms stems and
   pieces
1 10 3/4-ounce can cream of mushroom
   soup
3/4 teaspoon salt

Cook rice according to package directions. Brown sausage; drain fat. Sauté onions. Combine rice, onions, sausage and remaining ingredients; put in a 1-gallon bag and freeze.

To prepare for serving, thaw sausage and rice mixture. Put in a baking dish; bake uncovered in a preheated 350° oven for 1 hour. **Makes 6 servings.**

Summary of processes: Chop 1 1/4 cups onion, 1 cup green bell pepper, 1 cup celery

Freeze in: 1-gallon bag

Serve with: Cranberry Cream Salad (page 142), carrot and celery sticks

Note: This is quite spicy, so it isn't suitable for someone who is sick.

CHICKEN TETRAZZINI

1 16-ounce package (use half) spaghetti

1 ¼ cups finely chopped onion (1 cup sautéed)

3 tablespoons margarine

1 cup chopped green bell pepper

5 ½ cups cooked, diced chicken

4 cups grated Monterey Jack cheese

2 10 ¾-ounce cans cream of mushroom soup

1 10 ¾-ounce soup can milk

Salt and pepper to taste

Break spaghetti in half, and cook as directed on package until al dente; drain. Sauté onions in margarine. Thoroughly mix onions and remaining ingredients with spaghetti in a large bowl. Put spaghetti mixture in 2 containers, and freeze.

To prepare for serving, thaw tetrazzini and put in a baking dish. Bake uncovered in a preheated 350° oven until bubbly, about 30 to 40 minutes. **Makes 12 servings.**

Summary of processes: Dice 5 ½ cups cooked chicken; chop 1 cup green bell pepper, 1 ¼ cups onion; grate 4 cups Monterey Jack cheese

Freeze in: 2 6-cup containers

Serve with: Fresh Baked Asparagus (page 145), **Spring Cake** (page 141)

Note: Serve half the **Chicken Tetrazzini**; take the other half to a family with a new baby or a special need. Include applesauce and cake.

½ cup sugar

3 tablespoons cornstarch

½ cup white vinegar

1 8-ounce can pineapple chunks
  (reserve juice)

¼ cup soy sauce

½ teaspoon salt

1 teaspoon minced garlic (1 clove)

½ teaspoon paprika

½ teaspoon ground ginger

1 cup coarsely chopped celery

1 cup coarsely chopped onion

3 cups cooked, diced chicken

1 cup coarsely chopped green bell pepper

1 4-ounce can mushroom stems and
  pieces, drained

1 8-ounce can sliced water chestnuts,
  drained

2 cups regular, uncooked rice*

DEBORAH'S SWEET AND SOUR CHICKEN

In a medium saucepan, combine sugar and cornstarch; stir in white vinegar, juice from pineapple chunks, soy sauce, salt, garlic, paprika, ginger, celery and onion. Bring to a boil; reduce heat. Simmer, stirring constantly until thickened. Remove from heat. Stir in pineapple chunks, chicken, bell pepper, mushrooms and water chestnuts. Put in an 8-cup container and freeze.

To prepare for serving, thaw chicken and put in a baking dish treated with nonstick spray. Bake uncovered in a preheated 350° oven for 45 minutes. Prepare rice according to package directions. Serve chicken over rice. **Makes 8 servings.**

Summary of processes: Mince 1 clove garlic; coarsely chop 1 cup each onion, celery, bell pepper; dice 3 cups cooked chicken

Freeze in: 8-cup container

Serve with: Tossed green salad, dinner rolls

Note: If you want to fill the house with a good aroma, this is the dish! You can also substitute leftover cooked pork for the chicken.

LEMON CHICKEN

1 teaspoon dried thyme leaves
1 teaspoon salt
1/2 teaspoon pepper
1/8 teaspoon garlic powder

1/3 cup lemon juice
1 pound chicken pieces
1 cup regular, uncooked rice*

Mix all the spices and lemon juice in a 1-gallon bag, add chicken pieces, and freeze. When thawed, preheat oven to 450°. Arrange chicken skin-side down in a 8x8x2-inch baking dish treated with nonstick spray. Pour liquid over chicken. Bake 20 minutes. Turn chicken over, and baste it. Bake 15 to 20 minutes longer or until chicken is tender and no longer pink when cut along the bone. Prepare rice according to package directions. Serve chicken over rice. **Makes 4 servings.**

Freeze in: 1-gallon bag
Serve with: Cooked fresh broccoli, **Blueberry Pie** (page 140)

CHICKEN Á LA KING

1 strip diced bacon
1/4 cup finely chopped onion
1 2-ounce can mushroom stems and pieces (reserve 1/4 cup liquid)
1/4 cup chopped green bell pepper
1 tablespoon margarine or butter
1/4 cup all-purpose flour

1 teaspoon salt
1/4 teaspoon pepper
1 cup half-and-half
2/3 cup chicken broth
1 cup cooked, diced chicken
1 tablespoon pimientos
1 package patty shells*

In a large saucepan, cook and stir bacon, onion, mushrooms and bell pepper in margarine over medium heat until vegetables are tender. Blend in flour, salt and pepper. Cook over low heat, stirring constantly until well mixed.

Remove from heat. Stir in half-and-half, chicken broth and reserved mushroom liquid. Heat to a boil, stirring constantly for 1 minute. Stir in chicken and pimientos. Allow chicken mixture to cool, put in a 1-gallon bag, and freeze.

To prepare for serving, thaw patty shells and chicken sauce. Heat sauce in large saucepan until bubbly, stirring constantly. Serve in warmed patty shells. **Makes 4 to 5 servings.**

Summary of processes: Dice 1 strip bacon, 1 cup cooked chicken; chop 1/4 cup onion, 1/4 cup bell pepper
Freeze in: 1-gallon bag
Serve with: Fresh Baked Asparagus (page 145), red grapes or melon slices

1 10-ounce package frozen chopped broccoli
4 cups cooked, diced chicken
1 10 3/4-ounce can condensed cream of chicken soup
1/2 cup light mayonnaise
1 4-ounce can mushroom stems and pieces, drained
1/4 teaspoon curry powder
3/4 cup grated Parmesan cheese

Cook broccoli in boiling water according to package directions. Drain broccoli, and spread in a 13x9x2-inch baking dish. Mix chicken, soup, mayonnaise, mushrooms, curry powder and 1/2 cup Parmesan cheese in a medium bowl. Spread chicken mixture over broccoli. Sprinkle 1/4 cup Parmesan cheese over top. Cover dish with foil and freeze.

To prepare for serving, thaw dish, and bake covered in a preheated 350° oven for 40 minutes. Remove foil, stir to bring colder food in center to the outside; bake 20 minutes more. **Makes 6 servings.**

Summary of processes: Dice 4 cups cooked chicken

Freeze in: 13x9x2-inch baking dish

Serve with: Croissants, **Cranberry Cream Salad** (page 142)

4 boneless, skinless chicken breasts
Salt, pepper, paprika to taste
1 1/4 cups water or chicken broth
1 cup regular uncooked rice
1/2 envelope dry onion soup mix (1/4 cup)
1 10 3/4-ounce can condensed cream of mushroom soup
2 tablespoons pimientos (1/2 of a 2-ounce jar)

Sprinkle chicken breasts with salt, pepper and paprika. Mix chicken broth, uncooked rice, onion soup mix, cream soup and pimientos together; put in an 11x7x1 1/2-inch baking dish. Place chicken breasts on top of rice mixture. Cover dish with foil, and freeze.

To prepare for serving, thaw chicken dish. Bake uncovered in a preheated 375° oven 1 1/4 hours or until chicken and rice are tender. **Makes 4 servings.**

Freeze in: 11x7x1 1/2-inch baking dish

Serve with: **Marinated Veggies** (page 146), dinner rolls

ORIENTAL CHICKEN

2 tablespoons margarine
2 tablespoons all-purpose flour
1 cup chicken broth
1 cup water
1 tablespoon soy sauce

$1/2$ teaspoon garlic powder
2 cups cooked, diced chicken
$1/8$ teaspoon pepper
1 5-ounce can chow mein noodles*

Melt margarine in a medium saucepan over low heat. Add flour, and continue to stir over medium heat until bubbly. Add broth, water, soy sauce, garlic powder, chicken and pepper; simmer for 5 minutes. Cool and freeze in a 1-gallon bag.

To prepare for serving, thaw chicken. Heat in a pan until bubbly. Serve over chow mein noodles. **Makes 4 servings**.

Summary of processes: Dice 2 cups cooked chicken

Freeze in: 1-gallon bag

Serve with: Egg rolls, fortune cookies

SPLIT PEA SOUP

12 ounces dry, green split peas
3 cups water
$1/2$ pound cooked, cubed ham
$3/4$ teaspoon onion powder
$1/8$ teaspoon dried thyme leaves
$1/8$ teaspoon freshly ground pepper

$1/3$ cup chopped celery
$3/4$ cup peeled and sliced carrots
1 cup finely chopped onion
1 bay leaf
Salt to taste

Rinse split peas, soak them in cold water overnight; drain. Put peas with remaining ingredients in a large saucepan. Bring to a boil; reduce heat. Stirring occasionally, simmer about 2 hours until peas are tender and turn pasty. Cool and freeze in 6-cup container.

To serve, thaw peas, and simmer until warmed through. If peas are too thick, add water to make consistency of thick soup. **Makes 6 servings**.

Summary of processes: Soak split peas in water overnight; cut ham in cubes; peel and slice $3/4$ cup carrots; chop 1 cup onion, $3/4$ cup celery

Freeze in: 6-cup container

Serve with: Orange slices or canned peaches, cornbread

Ham Salad Filling

1 10-ounce package frozen peas (use half)
1 pound cooked, cubed ham (1 cup)
1/2 cup grated mild cheddar cheese
3/4 teaspoon prepared mustard
1 tablespoon minced onion
1/3 cup light mayonnaise*

Rinse peas under cold water to separate, but do not thaw; drain. Combine peas with ham, cheese, minced onion and mustard. Put in a 1-gallon freezer bag and freeze.

To prepare for serving, thaw ham salad filling, and make the following pastry:

Pastry*

1/3 cup plus 2 tablespoons water
2 tablespoons margarine
1/2 cup biscuit baking mix
2 eggs

Preheat oven to 400°. Spray an 8-inch pie plate with nonstick spray. Heat water and margarine to a boil in a 2-quart saucepan. Add baking mix all at once, stirring vigorously over low heat until mixture forms a ball, about 1 1/2 minutes. Remove from heat. Beat in eggs one at a time, and continue beating until smooth. Spread mixture in bottom of pie pan (not sides). Bake pastry uncovered until puffed and dry in center, about 35 to 40 minutes. Cool pastry. Just before serving, stir mayonnaise into cold ham mixture, fill pastry, and serve. **Makes 4 servings.**

Summary of processes: Cut 1 pound ham into cubes; grate 1/2 cup cheddar cheese

Freeze in: 1-gallon bag

Serve with: Lemon gelatin made with shredded carrots and crushed pineapple

CURRANT HAM LOAF

2 pounds cooked, ground ham (5 cups)
1 pound ground turkey
2 eggs
1 cup soda cracker crumbs

1 8-ounce can tomato sauce
2 tablespoons chili sauce (or use catsup)
1 10-ounce jar currant jelly*
1/2 6-ounce jar prepared mustard*

Combine ham, turkey, eggs, cracker crumbs, tomato sauce and chili sauce; form into a loaf. Put in 1-gallon bag or 9x5x3-inch loaf pan covered with foil and freeze.

To prepare for serving, thaw loaf. Bake uncovered in a preheated 350° oven for 1 1/2 hours. Combine jelly and mustard; pour over loaf. **Makes 6 servings.**

Summary of processes: Crush 1 cup soda crackers

Freeze in: 1-gallon bag or 9x5x3-inch loaf pan

Serve with: Cooked sweet potatoes glazed with orange juice and brown sugar, cooked green beans

MARINATED FLANK STEAK

1/2 cup vegetable oil
1/4 cup soy sauce
1/4 cup red wine vinegar
2 teaspoons Worcestershire sauce

1/2 teaspoon ground ginger
1 teaspoon minced garlic (1 clove)
1 1/3 pounds flank steak

Mix first six ingredients for marinade. Put flank steak in a freezer bag, pour marinade over it, seal bag, and freeze.

To prepare for serving, thaw flank steak, remove from marinade, and barbecue 8 to 10 minutes per side; or set oven control to broil and/or 550°. Broil steak 6 inches from heat until brown, turning once, about 6 minutes on one side and 4 minutes on the other. Cut steak across grain at slanted angle into thin slices. **Makes 4 servings.**

Summary of processes: Mince 1 clove garlic

Freeze in: 1-gallon bag

Serve with: Twice-Baked Potatoes Deluxe (page 145), cooked zucchini

2 pounds cubed, boneless, top sirloin
   steak
³/₄ cup coarsely chopped onion
1 4-ounce can green chili salsa
1 ¹/₂ teaspoons chili powder
1 tablespoon vegetable oil
¹/₄ cup red wine vinegar
¹/₄ teaspoon salt

Pepper to taste
¹/₂ green bell pepper*
1 onion*
4 ounces whole fresh mushrooms*
Half a pint box cherry tomatoes*
¹/₂ of 1 8-ounce can pineapple chunks
1 cup regular, uncooked rice*

Combine cubed beef with chopped onion, salsa, chili powder, oil, red wine vinegar, salt and pepper; put in a 6-cup container and freeze.

To prepare for serving, thaw meat mixture. Remove meat from marinade. Cut bell pepper and onion into thick pieces to put on a skewer. Alternate meat, vegetables and pineapple on a skewer, and barbecue or broil. Baste with marinade while cooking. At the same time, prepare rice according to package directions. Serve kebabs with rice.
Makes 4 servings.

Summary of processes: Cut steak into cubes; Chop ¹/₂ bell pepper and 1 ¹/₂ cups onion into thick pieces

Freeze in: 6-cup container

Serve with: Corn on the cob and **Spring Cake** (page 141)

Note: Serve these the first week; otherwise, fresh vegetables will spoil. You can also barbecue the kebabs.

GRILLED FISH

1 ¼ pounds frozen fish fillets (halibut, swordfish or orange roughy)*

5 to 6 new potatoes*

½ cup soy sauce

¼ cup water

¼ chicken bouillon cube

2 tablespoons olive oil

1 tablespoon brown sugar

2 teaspoons minced garlic (2 cloves)

½ teaspoon ground ginger

Freeze fish fillets, and store new potatoes until you're ready to serve them. Whisk remaining ingredients in a small bowl to make marinade. Freeze in a plastic bag taped to fish fillet package.

To prepare for serving, thaw marinade and fish fillets. Marinate fish 30 minutes. Prepare new potatoes. Heat 1 cup salted water to a boil; add potatoes. Cover, heat till boiling; reduce heat. Simmer tightly covered until tender, 30 to 35 minutes; drain.

At the same time, remove fish from marinade. Set oven control to broil and/or 550°. Broil or grill fish for 10 minutes per inch of thickness or until fish flakes easily with a fork. Baste frequently with marinade while cooking. If fish is more than 1-inch thick, turn once during cooking. **Makes 4 servings**.

Summary of processes: Mince 2 garlic cloves

Freeze in: 1-quart bag taped to fish fillet package

Serve with: Tossed green salad

1 10-ounce package frozen, chopped
  spinach
1 bunch chopped green onion bulbs
  (without greens)

4 eggs
1 16-ounce carton low-fat cottage cheese
2 cups grated, mild cheddar cheese
¼ cup crouton crumbs*

CRUSTLESS SPINACH QUICHE

Cook spinach according to package directions, and squeeze to remove liquid. Combine spinach, green onions, eggs, cottage cheese and cheddar cheese. Put into a quiche pan or 10-inch pie plate treated with nonstick spray. Cover with foil, and freeze. Put crouton crumbs in a 1-quart bag, and tape to pie plate.

To prepare for serving, thaw pie and crumbs. Bake uncovered in a preheated 325° oven for 1 hour, adding crouton crumbs the last 15 minutes. **Makes 8 servings.**

Summary of processes: Chop 1 bunch green onions; grate 2 cups cheddar cheese; crush croutons to make ¼ cup

Freeze in: 10-inch quiche pan or pie plate; 1-quart bag

Serve with: Fresh sliced tomatoes and **Cinnamon Logs** (page 137)

Note: This dish is nice for a ladies' luncheon.

1 2½-ounce package thin-sliced, corned
beef luncheon meat
1 8-ounce jar Cheez Whiz

1 tablespoon minced onion
2 tablespoons light mayonnaise
8 sandwich or onion rolls

JAN'S SANDWICHES

Chop corned beef and mix with Cheez Whiz, onion and mayonnaise. Spread filling on one bun; top with second bun. Wrap buns individually in foil, and freeze.

To prepare for serving, thaw rolls and bake in foil in a preheated 350° oven for 20 minutes. **Makes 8 servings.**

Summary of processes: Chop corned beef

Freeze in: Foil wrap

Serve with: Chips, fresh fruit salad

SAUCY HOT DOGS

2 cups Grandma's Chili*   6 hot dogs or turkey franks*
6 hot dog buns*

Thaw frozen chili, hot dogs and buns. Cook hot dogs in a small amount of water until heated through, drain, and cut lengthwise. Heat chili in a saucepan until bubbly. If desired, heat buns. Put hot dogs in buns, and smother with chili. **Makes 6 servings.**

Freeze in: 2-cup container

Serve with: Corn chips, cottage cheese, sliced pineapple and mandarin oranges

GRILLED HAM SLICES

2 pounds cut in 2 3/4-inch-thick center   1 tablespoon prepared mustard*
   slices of cooked ham*   2 teaspoons water*
1 cup regular, uncooked rice*   1 tablespoon vinegar or lemon juice*
3/4 cup brown sugar*

Freeze ham slices in 1-gallon bag.
To serve, thaw ham slices. Prepare rice according to package directions. Mix remaining ingredients for glaze, and spread over ham slices. Grill, broil or barbeque ham slices 2 or 3 minutes per side, basting with sauce once per side. **Makes 4 servings.**

Freeze in: 1-gallon bag

Serve with: Cinnamon Applesauce Salad (page 142), **Swedish Rye Bread** (page 136)

2 ½ pounds chicken pieces*
½ cup grated, mild cheddar cheese*

1 cup barbecue sauce (favorite)*
1 10-ounce tube Hungry Jack Biscuits*

Freeze chicken in a 1-gallon bag and cheddar cheese in a 1-quart bag. Refrigerate sauce and biscuits until serving day.

To serve, thaw chicken and grated cheese. Preheat oven to 400°. Treat a 13x9x2-inch baking dish with nonstick spray. Dip chicken pieces in barbecue sauce. Place them in pan, skin side up. Bake 40 to 45 minutes. Pile chicken pieces at one end of pan. Separate dough into 10 biscuits. Place them in the pan in drippings next to chicken. Sprinkle cheese over biscuits. Bake 15 to 20 minutes until biscuits are golden brown. **Makes 5 servings.**

Summary of processes: Grate ½ cup cheddar cheese

Freeze in: 1-gallon and 1-quart bags

Serve with: Baked beans, cole slaw

OVEN BARBECUED CHICKEN AND CHEESY BISCUITS

CHAPTER 5

"He makes grass grow for the cattle, and plants for man to cultivate—bringing forth food from the earth"

(Psalm 104:14, NIV).

MENU CALENDAR

SUN.	MON.	TUES.	WED.	THURS.	FRI.	SAT.
	1 Eat Out Cooking Day!	**2** Hearty Hamburger Tomato Stew	**3** Chinese Chicken Morsels	**4** Veggie Pizza	**5** Grilled Fish	**6** Chicken Spaghetti
7 Mandarin Orange Chicken	**8** Vegetable Lasagna	**9** Stove-Top Barbecued Chicken	**10** Split Pea Soup	**11** Blackened Chicken Breast	**12** Chicken Cacciatore	**13** Pizza Roll-Ups
14 Savory Beef	**15** Chili Verde					

GROCERY SHOPPING AND STAPLES LISTS

An asterisk (*) after an item indicates that it should be stored until you cook the dish it will be served with. For example, the corn tortillas and salsa will not be used until the day you serve **Chili Verde**. Mark those items as a reminder that you will need them for an entrée.

When entrées require perishable foods to be refrigerated until served, you may want to prepare those dishes right away or buy the food the week you plan to make the dish. For example, fresh mushrooms would spoil by the end of a month.

For the low-fat entrée plan, you will need these food items as well as the ones in the staples list that follows:

Canned Goods
1 16-ounce can corn
1 4-ounce can chopped green chilies
1 16-ounce can cut green beans
1 8-ounce bottle lemon juice (1/2 cup)
1 11-ounce can mandarin orange sections*
1 8-ounce can sliced mushrooms
1 3-ounce can sliced ripe olives
1 2-ounce jar pimientos
1 11 1/2-ounce jar salsa*
1 46-ounce can tomato juice
1 6-ounce can tomato paste
5 28-ounce cans Italian-style or plain crushed tomatoes in puree

Grains, Noodles and Rice
1 8-ounce package lasagna
1 8-ounce package dry pinto beans
1 16-ounce package regular rice (1 cup*)
6 sandwich rolls*
1 12-ounce package spaghetti

1 packet dry spaghetti sauce seasoning mix
1 8-ounce package wide egg noodles
1 16-ounce package spinach or wide egg noodles
1 12-ounce package dry, green split peas
1 dozen corn tortillas*

Frozen Foods
1 1/4 pounds frozen fish fillets (halibut, swordfish or orange roughy)*
2 loaves frozen French, pizza, Italian or all-purpose bread dough or **Dawn's French Bread** (page 135).
1 6-ounce can frozen orange juice concentrate

Dairy Products
8 ounces low-fat cheddar cheese
4 ounces reduced fat Monterey Jack cheese
15 ounces part-skim mozzarella cheese
16 ounces low-fat ricotta cheese

109

Meat and Poultry
2 pounds chicken pieces
7 pounds boneless, skinless chicken
    breasts
2 pounds lean ground beef or turkey
2 pounds beef round tip steak
1/2 pound cooked turkey ham

Produce
3 green bell peppers
1 small red bell pepper
2 medium stalks fresh broccoli
5 carrots (2 3/4 cups sliced)

1 bunch celery
4 cloves garlic
1 3/4 pounds fresh mushrooms (8 cups
    sliced)
1 bunch green onions
3 pounds brown or yellow onions
    (6 medium)
1 bunch fresh parsley
5 or 6 new potatoes
1 medium zucchini
Make sure you have the following staples
on hand; add those you don't have to the
above shopping list:

STAPLES LIST

dried basil leaves
bay leaf
beef bouillon cubes (2)
brown sugar
catsup (1/3 cup)
celery seed
chicken bouillon cubes (6)
chili powder
ground cloves
ground cumin
Dijon mustard (1/4 cup)
dill weed
dry mustard

all-purpose flour
garlic powder
garlic salt
ground ginger
Italian seasoning
light mayonnaise
low-fat margarine
nonstick spray
olive oil
onion powder
dried oregano leaves
paprika
Parmesan cheese
pepper: cayenne, white, freshly ground
black and regular black
soy sauce (3/4 cup)
sugar
dried thyme leaves
vegetable oil (about 1/2 cup)
white vinegar
Worcestershire sauce (about 3 tablespoons)

The following list of freezer containers or flat baking dishes will be needed for the entrées in the two-week cycle. They're not the only containers in which you could freeze these foods, but the list gives you an idea of the size and number of containers you'll need.

1 empty spice jar or small container:
Blackened Chicken

5 1-gallon freezer bags:
Pizza Roll-Ups, 4; **Chinese Chicken Morsels**

8 1-quart freezer bags:
Pizza Roll-Ups, 4; **Grilled Fish**; **Blackened Chicken**; **Chicken Spaghetti**; **Chili Verde**

Heavy aluminum foil:
Veggie Pizza; **Vegetable Lasagna**

1 12-inch pizza pan or 10-inch pie plate:
Veggie Pizza

2 4-cup freezer containers:
Stove-Top Barbecued Chicken; **Mandarin Orange Chicken**

1 5-cup freezer container:
Chili Verde

1 6-cup freezer container:
Split Pea Soup

1 8-cup freezer container:
Savory Beef

2 16-cup freezer containers:
Hearty Hamburger Tomato Stew; **Chicken Spaghetti**

2 13x9x2-inch baking dishes:
Vegetable Lasagna; **Chicken Cacciatore**

FREEZER CONTAINERS

THE DAY BEFORE COOKING DAY

1. Freeze fish fillets, sandwich rolls and 1 1/2-pounds boneless, skinless chicken breasts for **Blackened Chicken Breasts**. Refrigerate 2 pounds chicken.

2. Use kitchen scissors or knife to cut 2 pounds raw, boneless chicken breasts into 1-inch cubes for **Mandarin Orange Chicken** and **Chinese Chicken Morsels**; refrigerate until needed.

3. In a large skillet, sauté remaining 3 1/2-pounds boneless, skinless chicken breasts in a small amount of water until no longer pink in the center. Use kitchen scissors or knife to cut cooled chicken into 1-inch cubes. Store chicken in the refrigerator.

4. Set out appliances, bowls, canned goods, dry ingredients, freezer containers and recipes.

5. Thaw 3 loaves of frozen bread dough in refrigerator overnight.

6. Rinse green split peas, and soak them covered with cold water overnight. Do the same for pinto beans.

Make sure you've cleared the table and counters of unnecessary kitchenware to allow plenty of working room. It also helps to have fresh, damp washcloths and towels for wiping your hands and the cooking area. The day will go smoother if you keep cleaning and organizing as you work.

Before you prepare a recipe, gather all the spices and ingredients in the assembly area to save time and steps. When you finish the recipe, remove unneeded items, and wipe off the work space.

Slightly undercook regular rice and noodles (al dente) that will be frozen. When you reheat them, they will have a better consistency and won't turn mushy.

Before Assembling Dishes:

1. Put out 6-ounce can of frozen orange juice concentrate to thaw.

2. Brown 2 pounds of ground beef or turkey, drain, and blot on a paper towel.

3. Perform all chopping, grating and slicing tasks.
Turkey ham: Cut into cubes.
Beef: Slice round tip steak into strips about 2 inches long.
Onions: Slice 2 onions; chop the rest.
Green onions: Chop onion bulbs only; discard green tops.
Broccoli: Chop fine 2 florets with small amount of stalks.

Carrots: Slice 2 3/4 cups.
Celery: Chop 1 1/3 cups and slice 3 stalks, storing them in separate small bags.
Garlic: Mince 4 cloves.
Mushrooms: Slice all (8 cups).
Parsley: Chop the whole bunch.
Green bell peppers: Chop 2, slice 1/2.
Red bell pepper: Chop 1/2 cup.
Zucchini: Chop 1 cup.
Mozzarella, cheddar and Monterey Jack cheeses: Grate all; put in separate bags.

4. Treat baking dishes and pie or pizza pans you will need with nonstick spray (check list of freezer containers on page 111).

5. As you assemble each group of the following entrées, allow them to cool if necessary, put them in storage containers and freeze.

Assemble Group 1 Entrées

1. Combine ingredients for **Italian Tomato Sauce**, and start it simmering.

2. Assemble and bake **Veggie Pizza**.

3. Roll out dough for **Pizza Roll-Ups**. Assemble and bake them.

4. Mix ingredients for **Hearty Hamburger Tomato Stew**, and start it simmering.

5. As soon as the above dishes are completed and have cooled, label each one and freeze.

Assemble Group 2 Entrées

1. Cook lasagna and broccoli for **Vegetable Lasagna**, and then finish assembling it.

2. Make marinade for **Grilled Fish**.

3. Label and freeze these dishes.

Assemble Group 3 Entrées

1. Assemble and start cooking **Split Pea Soup** and **Chili Verde**.

2. Complete **Savory Beef** in a skillet. Allow to cool, label and freeze.

Assemble Group 4 Entrées

1. Make **Stove-Top Barbecued Chicken** in one large skillet or pan with lid and **Chicken Cacciatore** in another.

2. While these are simmering, assemble **Chinese Chicken Morsels.**

3. Mix spices for **Blackened Chicken Breasts**.

4. Prepare **Mandarin Orange Chicken**.

5. Assemble **Chicken Spaghetti**, cooking noodles while chicken and tomato sauce are simmering.

6. Complete **Split Pea Soup** and **Chili Verde**; allow to cool.

7. Label and freeze this last batch of dishes.

Take a minute to enjoy looking into your freezer at all the food you've prepared!

RECIPES FOR THE LOW-FAT ENTRÉE PLAN

Each recipe offers complete instructions on how to prepare the dish. Food items with an asterisk (*) won't be prepared until you serve the entrée. For recipes calling for oven baking, preheat oven for about 10 minutes.

"Summary of processes" gives a quick overview of foods that need to be chopped, diced, grated or sliced. "Freeze in" tells what bags and containers will be needed to freeze each entrée. "Serve with" offers suggestions of foods to accompany the meal. Some of the recipes for those foods are included in chapter 6; page numbers are indicated for easy reference. "Note" includes special instructions on how the entrée can be used in other ways.

ITALIAN TOMATO SAUCE

3 28-ounce cans Italian-style or plain crushed tomatoes in puree
3 tablespoons sugar
3 tablespoons Italian seasoning
6 tablespoons chopped, fresh parsley
3 tablespoons dried basil leaves
3 teaspoons garlic salt
1 1/2 teaspoons pepper

Mix all the ingredients in a heavy, large pot. Bring to a boil; reduce heat. Simmer 15 minutes, stirring occasionally. Save 4 1/2 cups sauce for **Vegetable Lasagna** and 1 cup for **Veggie Pizza**. Divide remaining sauce into four 1-cup portions, and put in four 1-quart bags for **Pizza Roll-Ups. Makes 9 1/2 cups.**

Summary of Processes: Chop 6 tablespoons parsley

Freeze in: 4 1-quart bags

VEGGIE PIZZA

1/4 cup chopped onion
1/4 cup chopped red bell pepper
1/4 cup chopped green bell pepper
1 cup chopped zucchini
1 cup sliced fresh mushrooms
1 tablespoon vegetable oil
1/2 cup grated part-skim mozzarella cheese
1 loaf frozen French, pizza, Italian or all-purpose bread dough or Dawn's French Bread (page 135).
1 cup Italian Tomato Sauce

Sauté vegetables in oil, drain well, and allow to cool. Stir in cheese. Roll dough into a 1/2-inch-thick circle. Put dough on a 12-inch pizza pan or 10-inch pie plate. Spread **Italian Tomato Sauce** on pizza. Spoon vegetable mixture over sauce. Bake pizza at 400° for 20 minutes. Cool, cover pizza with heavy aluminum foil and freeze.

To prepare for serving, thaw and then heat pizza in a pre-heated 400° oven for about 20 minutes. **Makes 6 servings.**

Summary of processes: Chop 1/4 cup onion, 1/4 cup red bell pepper, 1/4 cup green bell pepper, 1 cup zucchini; slice 1 cup fresh mushrooms; grate 1/2 cup part-skim mozzarella cheese

Freeze in: 12-inch pizza pan or 10-inch pie pan; heavy aluminum foil

Serve with: Lemon gelatin with pears

Note: A tasty addition to this pizza is 1/2 pound browned turkey sausage, 1 teaspoon parsley, 1 teaspoon dried basil leaves, 1 teaspoon dried oregano leaves and 1/2 teaspoon salt.

1 loaf frozen French, pizza, Italian or all-purpose bread dough, or Dawn's French Bread (page 135).

1 pound lean ground beef or turkey (2 1/2 cups browned)

1 teaspoon salt

1/2 teaspoon pepper

2 cups grated part-skim mozzarella cheese

1 teaspoon Italian seasoning

1 tablespoon chopped fresh parsley

4 cups Italian Tomato Sauce*

Thaw dough; roll it into a 14x24-inch rectangle about 1/4-inch thick. Brown ground beef or turkey; stir in remaining ingredients. Spoon filling evenly onto dough, slightly pressing filling into dough.

Roll dough lengthwise like a jelly roll, and cut into 24 1-inch slices. Treat 2 rimmed cookie sheets with nonstick spray; lay slices on sheets about an inch apart. Preheat oven to 400°. Let roll-ups sit for 10 minutes. Bake for 20 to 25 minutes or till golden brown. Cool roll-ups, and freeze in 4 1-gallon bags, 6 per bag. Slip a 1-quart bag with 1 cup sauce into each bag of **Pizza Roll-Ups**.

To prepare, thaw roll-ups, and warm them in a pre-heated 400° oven for 10 minutes. Or put them frozen in the microwave; heat on high for about 2 minutes. Serve with warmed **Italian Tomato Sauce. Makes 24 servings**.

Summary of processes: Chop 1 tablespoon parsley; grate 2 cups part-skim mozzarella cheese

Freeze in: 4 1-gallon bags, **Roll-Ups**; 4 1-quart bags, **Italian Tomato Sauce**

Serve with: Tossed green salad

Note: These roll-ups are super for picnics or nights when the family must eat in shifts. They can be eaten warm or cold. They're also a favorite with kids and an easy snack.

HEARTY HAMBURGER TOMATO STEW

1 pound lean ground beef or turkey (2 ½ cups browned)
1 ¼ cups chopped onion
2 cups peeled and sliced carrots
1 cup chopped green bell pepper
1 cup sliced fresh mushrooms
1 16-ounce can cut green beans, drained
1 16-ounce can corn, drained
3 stalks sliced celery
1 46-ounce can tomato juice
2 teaspoons sugar
1 teaspoon celery seed
Salt and pepper to taste

Brown ground beef or turkey in a large saucepan. Mix in remaining ingredients; bring to a boil; reduce heat. Simmer covered 30 minutes, stirring occasionally. Cool and freeze.

To prepare for serving, thaw stew. Then bring to a boil; reduce heat; simmer 10 minutes. **Makes 8 servings**.

Summary of processes: Chop 1 ¼ cups onion and 1 cup green bell pepper; peel and slice 2 cups carrots, 1 cup fresh mushrooms, 3 stalks celery

Freeze in: 16-cup container

Serve with: Cornbread or wheat crackers

1 8-ounce package lasagna
2 stalks finely chopped broccoli florets
1 16-ounce carton low-fat ricotta cheese
1 cup grated part-skim mozzarella
cheese
1 8-ounce can sliced mushrooms,
drained
2 chopped green onion bulbs (without
greens)

2 teaspoons dried basil leaves
1 1/2 teaspoons crumbled dried oregano
leaves
1/4 cup finely chopped fresh parsley
Dash of fresh ground black pepper
3 1/2 cups Italian Tomato Sauce

Boil lasagna 10 minutes or until al dente, stirring occasionally to prevent noodles from sticking. Drain noodles, rinse in cold water, and then lay them next to each other on waxed paper to dry. Cook broccoli 5 minutes in boiling water.

Combine cheeses, vegetables, herbs and pepper in a medium bowl. In a 13x9x2-inch dish, layer lasagna noodles, spread with half the cheese mixture and half the tomato sauce. Repeat process, topping with noodles and covering with sauce. Wrap dish with foil and freeze.

To prepare for serving, thaw dish. Preheat oven to 350°. Bake covered for 20 minutes. Remove foil, and bake 15 to 20 minutes more until heated through. **Makes 12 servings**.

Summary of processes: Grate 1 cup part-skim mozzarella cheese; chop 2 small broccoli stalks, 2 green onion bulbs, 1/4 cup parsley

Freeze in: 13x9x2-inch baking dish

Serve with: Fresh fruit salad, bread sticks

Note: For an alternate way to prepare this entrée, use large shell pasta. Cook pasta as directed on package until al dente. Stuff each shell with cheese mixture. Freeze stuffed shells on a rimmed baking sheet. When they're hard, transfer them to a freezer bag. Freeze sauce in a separate bag taped to pasta bag. Thaw number of shells and amount of sauce desired. Warm them in a pre-heated 350° oven about 20 minutes. Serve shells with warmed sauce poured over them.

GRILLED FISH

1 ¼ pounds frozen fish fillets (halibut, swordfish or orange roughy)*

5 to 6 new potatoes*

½ cup soy sauce

¼ cup water

¼ chicken bouillon cube

2 tablespoons olive oil

1 tablespoon brown sugar

2 teaspoons minced garlic (2 cloves)

½ teaspoon ground ginger

Freeze fish fillets, and store new potatoes until you're ready to serve them. Whisk remaining ingredients in a small bowl to make marinade. Freeze in a plastic bag taped to fish fillet package.

To prepare for serving, thaw marinade and fish fillets. Marinate fish 30 minutes. Prepare new potatoes. Heat 1 cup salted water to a boil; add potatoes. Cover, heat till boiling; then reduce heat. Simmer tightly covered until tender, 30 to 35 minutes; drain.

At the same time, remove fish from marinade. Set oven control to broil and/or 550°. Broil or grill fish for 10 minutes per inch of thickness or until fish flakes easily with a fork. Baste frequently with marinade while cooking. If fish is more than 1-inch thick, turn once during cooking. **Makes 4 servings**.

Summary of processes: Mince 2 garlic cloves

Freeze in: 1-quart bag taped to fish fillet package

Serve with: Tossed green salad

1 12-ounce package dry, green split peas
3 cups water
1/2 pound cooked, cubed turkey ham
3/4 teaspoon onion powder
1/8 teaspoon dried thyme leaves
1/8 teaspoon freshly ground pepper

1/3 cup chopped celery
3/4 cup peeled and sliced carrots
1 cup chopped onion
1 bay leaf
Salt to taste

SPLIT PEA SOUP

Rinse split peas, soak them in cold water overnight; drain. Put peas with remaining ingredients in a large saucepan. Bring to a boil; reduce heat. Stirring occasionally, simmer about 2 hours until peas are tender and turn pasty. Cool and freeze.

To serve, thaw peas and simmer until warmed through. If peas are too condensed, add water to make consistency of thick soup. **Makes 6 servings**.

Summary of processes: Soak split peas in water overnight; cut ham into cubes; peel and slice 3/4 cup carrots; chop 1 cup onion, 1/3 cup celery

Freeze in: 6-cup container

Serve with: Orange slices or canned peaches, cornbread

CHILI VERDE

1 8-ounce package dry pinto beans (1 1/4 cups)

1 pound boneless, skinless chicken breasts (2 cups cooked)

1 4-ounce can chopped green chilies

1 teaspoon ground cumin

3/4 teaspoon dried oregano leaves

1/8 teaspoon ground cloves

1/8 teaspoon cayenne pepper

3 cups water

3 chicken bouillon cubes

1 teaspoon minced garlic (1 clove)

1 teaspoon salt

2/3 cup finely chopped onion

1 cup grated low-fat Monterey Jack cheese*

1 dozen corn tortillas*

1 11 1/2-ounce jar salsa*

Rinse pinto beans, soak them in cold water overnight, then drain them. Cut chicken into 1-inch cubes; cook until no longer pink in small amount of water or vegetable oil. Combine chicken with chilies and seasonings; refrigerate until needed. At the same time, combine beans, water, bouillon cubes, garlic, salt and onion in a large pot; bring to a boil. Reduce heat and simmer until beans are soft, about 1 hour. Add more water if necessary.

Combine chicken and spices with beans; simmer 10 more minutes. Cool and freeze. Grate cheese, put it in a 1-quart bag, and attach it to the freezer container with the chili.

To serve, thaw chili and cheese. Simmer chili 30 minutes, stirring occasionally. Top chili with salsa and grated cheese; serve on warmed corn tortillas. **Makes 5 servings.**

Summary of processes: Soak 1/2 pound pinto beans overnight; chop 2 cups cooked chicken, 2/3 cup onion; grate 1 cup low-fat Monterey Jack cheese

Freeze in: 5-cup container; 1-quart bag

Serve with: Tossed green salad

2 pounds beef round tip steak

Freshly ground black pepper to taste

1 cup sliced fresh mushrooms

1 sliced onion

3 tablespoons vegetable oil

3 tablespoons all-purpose flour

2 cups water

2 beef bouillon cubes

2 tablespoons tomato paste

1 teaspoon dry mustard

1/4 teaspoon dried oregano leaves

1/4 teaspoon dill weed

2 tablespoons Worcestershire sauce

1 8-ounce package wide egg noodles*

SAVORY BEEF

Cut beef into thin strips about 2 inches long. Sprinkle beef with pepper, and set meat aside in a cool place. In a heavy skillet, sauté mushrooms and onions in oil until golden; remove them from skillet. Put meat in same skillet; cook and stir steak quickly on all sides until it's brown but still rare in the center. Remove meat, and set aside.

Blend flour into the oil in skillet, gradually adding water and beef bouillon. Stir constantly until smooth and slightly thick. Mix in tomato paste, dry mustard, oregano, dill weed and Worcestershire sauce. Stir meat, mushrooms and onions into sauce. Cool meat mixture and freeze.

To prepare for serving, thaw beef. Prepare noodles according to package directions. Heat beef in a saucepan over medium heat, stirring constantly until it's bubbly. Serve meat over noodles. **Makes 6 servings.**

Summary of processes: Slice 1 cup fresh mushrooms and 1 onion

Freeze in: 8-cup container

Serve with: French-cut green beans

Note: Use any leftover beef for sandwiches.

STOVE-TOP BARBEQUED CHICKEN

1 teaspoon vegetable oil
1 cup finely chopped onion
1/3 cup catsup
1/3 cup water
4 teaspoons white vinegar
4 teaspoons brown sugar

1 1/2 teaspoons Worcestershire sauce
1/2 teaspoon chili powder
1/4 teaspoon crushed celery seeds
2 pounds skinned chicken pieces
1 16-ounce package spinach or
wide egg noodles (use half)*

Heat oil in a large, nonstick skillet; sauté onion until tender. Stir in catsup, water, vinegar, brown sugar, Worcestershire sauce, chili powder and celery seeds. Bring sauce to a boil. Add the chicken to the skillet, placing the side down that has the skin removed; spoon sauce over the pieces. Bring to a boil; reduce heat. Cover and simmer 30 minutes. Turn chicken pieces, and simmer covered for about 20 minutes more or until chicken is cooked through. Cool and freeze chicken and sauce.

To prepare for serving, thaw chicken and sauce; put in a large skillet, and cook over medium heat, stirring constantly until bubbly. Cook half package of spinach or egg noodles according to directions; serve chicken over noodles. **Makes 4 servings.**

Summary of processes: Chop 1 cup onion

Freeze in: 4-cup container

Serve with: Corn on the cob, **Low-Calorie Chocolate Cake** (page 140)

1 pound boneless, skinless chicken breasts (2 cups cooked)
1 tablespoon vegetable oil
1 sliced medium onion
1/2 sliced green bell pepper
2 cups sliced fresh mushrooms
1 teaspoon minced garlic (1 clove)
1 28-ounce can Italian-style or plain crushed tomatoes in puree

2 tablespoons chopped fresh parsley
1 teaspoon salt
1/4 teaspoon pepper
2 teaspoons Italian seasoning
1 teaspoon dried basil leaves
Parmesan cheese*
1 16-ounce package spinach or wide egg noodles (use half)*

Cut chicken into 1-inch cubes. In a large skillet, sauté chicken in vegetable oil until no longer pink in the center. Remove chicken from skillet and sauté onion, green bell pepper, mushrooms and garlic until onion is transparent. Add chicken and remaining ingredients except Parmesan cheese and noodles to the skillet. Simmer 15 minutes. Allow sauce to cool, put in a 13x9x2-inch baking dish, cover with foil and freeze.

To serve, thaw dish, and bake chicken in a preheated oven at 350° for 35 minutes. Cook half package spinach or egg noodles according to directions. Serve chicken over noodles, and sprinkle on Parmesan cheese. **Makes 6 servings**.

Summary of processes: Cut 1 pound chicken into cubes; slice 1 medium onion, 1/2 green bell pepper, 2 cups fresh mushrooms; mince 1 clove garlic

Freeze in: 13x9x2-inch baking dish

Serve with: Cooked baby carrots, **Dawn's French Bread** (page 135)

CHINESE CHICKEN MORSELS

1 pound boneless, skinless chicken breasts (2 cups)
½ cup lemon juice
¼ cup soy sauce
¼ cup Dijon mustard
2 teaspoons vegetable oil
¼ teaspoon cayenne pepper
1 cup regular, uncooked rice*

Cut chicken breasts (kitchen scissors work best) into 1-inch cubes. Mix lemon juice, soy sauce, mustard, oil and pepper. Put marinade and chicken cubes in a 1-gallon bag, and store in the freezer.

To prepare for serving, thaw chicken and remove from marinade. Warm marinade in a small saucepan. Place cubes about an inch apart on broiler pan treated with nonstick spray. Broil 4 to 5 inches from heat for 7 minutes, brushing with marinade once. Turn chicken cubes, and broil another 4 minutes. Meanwhile, prepare rice according to package directions. Heat remaining marinade and serve over rice. **Makes 4 to 5 servings.**

Summary of processes: Cut chicken into 1-inch cubes

Freeze in: 1-gallon bag

Serve with: Sliced, fresh tomatoes or tossed salad, **Spicy Pumpkin Muffins** (page 137)

Note: For a luncheon alternative, toss sautéed or broiled chicken morsels with mixed salad greens, shredded carrots, cherry tomatoes, chopped green bell pepper, sliced water chestnuts and croutons. Use your favorite low-calorie dressing.

1 1/2 pounds boneless, skinless chicken breasts*
6 sandwich rolls*

1 tablespoon vegetable oil*
Low-fat margarine or light mayonnaise*
1/4 cup melted low-fat margarine*

Spice Mix*
2 teaspoons paprika
1 teaspoon onion powder
1 teaspoon garlic powder
1/4 teaspoon cayenne pepper

1/2 teaspoon white pepper
1/2 teaspoon black pepper
1/2 teaspoon salt
1/2 teaspoon dried thyme leaves
1/2 teaspoon dried oregano leaves

Freeze chicken and sandwich rolls until ready to serve. Mix spices; store in a covered container such as an empty spice jar, which you've labeled "**Blackened Chicken Spices**."

To serve, thaw rolls and chicken. Coat each piece of chicken with about 1 tablespoon spice mix. The mixture is hot and spicy, so adjust amount for taste of each person. Using a pastry brush, baste each piece of chicken with melted, low-fat margarine. Grill chicken, basting with low-fat margarine after turning once. Grill about 10 minutes or until no longer pink in the middle. Or cook chicken in a large, nonstick skillet in hot oil over medium heat. Cook, turning chicken once, until it's done, about 10 minutes. Serve on sandwich rolls spread with a little margarine or light mayonnaise. **Makes 6 servings**.

Summary of processes: Mix spices

Freeze in: 1-quart bag

Serve with: Applesauce, carrot and celery strips

Note: Use spice mix on your favorite fish fillets.

MANDARIN ORANGE CHICKEN

1 pound boneless, skinless chicken breasts (2 cups cooked)
1 tablespoon vegetable oil
2 cups sliced, fresh mushrooms
2 teaspoons all-purpose flour
2/3 cup water
1 6-ounce can frozen orange juice
concentrate, thawed
1/2 cup thinly sliced green onion bulbs (without greens)
2 chicken bouillon cubes
1 11-ounce can mandarin orange sections, drained*
1 cup regular, uncooked rice*

Cut chicken into 1-inch chunks with kitchen scissors or knife. Heat oil in large skillet; add chicken, and cook on medium high until browned on both sides. Remove and set aside chicken. In the same skillet, cook mushrooms over medium high, stirring constantly. Sprinkle flour over mushrooms, stirring quickly to combine. Gradually stir in water, orange juice concentrate, green onions and bouillon cubes. Stirring constantly, bring to a boil. Reduce heat, add chicken, and let simmer 3 to 4 minutes. Cool and freeze.

To serve, thaw chicken mixture, and cook rice according to package directions. Heat chicken mixture in a saucepan until bubbly, stir in drained orange segments and heat through. Combine with cooked rice and serve. **Makes 4 servings.**

Summary of processes: Cut 1 pound chicken into chunks; slice 2 cups fresh mushrooms, 1/2 cup green onion bulbs

Freeze in: 4-cup container

Serve with: French-cut green beans, biscuits

1 12-ounce package spaghetti (semolina)
1 1/2 pounds boneless, skinless chicken
   breasts (3 cups cooked)
1 28-ounce can Italian-style or plain
   crushed tomatoes in puree
1 2-ounce jar pimentos
1 cup chopped green bell pepper

1 cup chopped celery
1 cup sliced fresh mushrooms
1 1/2 cups chopped onion
1 3-ounce can sliced ripe olives
1 packet dry spaghetti sauce seasoning
Salt and pepper to taste
2 cups grated low-fat cheddar cheese*

Cook spaghetti until al dente; drain. At the same time, cut chicken into 1-inch cubes; cook chicken in a small amount of water until no longer pink in the center. In a large pot, combine chicken with remaining ingredients except cheese. Bring mixture to a boil; reduce heat. Simmer for 15 minutes, stirring occasionally. Add cooked spaghetti to sauce. Cool and freeze in 16-cup container; tape 1-quart bag with cheese to container.

To prepare for serving, thaw cheese and spaghetti. Bake spaghetti in a preheated 325° oven for 40 minutes. Top spaghetti with cheese; return spaghetti to oven for 5 minutes or until cheese melts. **Makes 10 servings.**

Summary of processes: Cut 1 1/2 pounds chicken into 1-inch cubes; chop 1 cup green bell pepper, 1 cup celery and 1 1/2 cups onion; slice 1 cup fresh mushrooms; grate 2 cups low-fat cheddar cheese

Freeze in: 16-cup container; 1-quart bag

Serve with: Tossed green salad, **Dawn's French Bread** (page 135)

CHAPTER 6

"They broke bread in their homes and ate together with glad and sincere hearts, praising God and enjoying the favor of all the people"

(Acts 2:46b-47, NIV).

BREADS AND GRAINS

Bread baking can be rewarding and fun, but never try it on cooking day. Mimi likes to bake bread once a week. She may bake whole wheat bread and cinnamon or dinner rolls one week, and the next raisin bread and muffins. She makes enough to store some in the freezer, which means a nice variety is always on hand.

For successful yeast breads, follow these suggestions. Whenever possible, use honey instead of sugar. Honey has more nutritional value and helps keep the bread moist. Try a heavy-duty mixer with a hook to knead the dough. If you knead it by hand, fold dough, push it with the heels of your hands, and turn it slightly, repeating until dough is smooth and elastic.

Allow bread to rise in a warm but not hot place. If it's a cold day, put bowl on the clothes dryer or by a heat vent. An unheated oven also works well. Put a pan of hot water on a lower rack under the bowl or pans containing the dough (making sure you remove them before preheating the oven).

We also recommend you bake the loaves before freezing them. Then wrap them carefully; a hole in the foil or freezer bag causes bread to dry out quickly.

We've included our favorite bread, granola and muffin recipes here for your baking pleasure. Following the breads and grains section, you will also find recipes for beverages, desserts, salads, sauces, soups and vegetables.

1 package active dry yeast
3 cups lukewarm water
1 cup powdered milk
1/2 cup honey
4 cups whole wheat flour (or substitute
  1 cup wheat germ for 1 cup whole

wheat flour)
1 1/2 tablespoons salt
1/2 cup vegetable oil
5 to 6 cups all-purpose flour
Melted butter or margarine

In a large mixing bowl, dissolve yeast in lukewarm water. Add milk and honey and then 4 cups whole wheat flour. Beat with a whisk until lumps disappear (it will be about as thick as cake batter). Cover bowl with a towel, and let dough rise 60 minutes or until double.

Add salt and vegetable oil; beat in white flour, working all of it in until it's no longer sticky. Knead with a dough hook 3 to 4 minutes or 10 minutes by hand, until dough is smooth. Put dough in a large, greased bowl, turning it once so it's greased on the top and bottom. Cover bowl with a towel, and let dough rise 50 minutes or until double.

Punch dough down, and let it rise 40 more minutes or until double. Divide dough in half, and shape into 2 large, smooth loaves. Grease pans with vegetable shortening, and put loaves in pans. Cover pans with a towel, and let dough rise 30 minutes or until double. Set timer for 15 minutes to remind yourself to preheat oven to 350°. Bake one hour. Remove loaves from oven; brush tops with melted butter or margarine. **Makes 2 loaves.**

Dinner Rolls: Divide dough in half, making one half into a loaf. Make dinner rolls out of the other half by rolling dough into a long tube about 2 inches thick. Cut the tube at 2-inch intervals; roll each piece into a round ball. Bake rolls on a cookie sheet in a preheated oven at 350° for 25 to 30 minutes. Rub a cube of butter over the tops of warm rolls.

Cheddar-Beef Rolls: Form dough into balls according to the above directions; then flatten balls into circles about the size of your palm. Fold each circle of dough around a small wedge of cheddar cheese and 2 tablespoons browned ground beef. Preheat oven to 350°. Bake sealed-side down on a cookie sheet 25 to 30 minutes. Put barbecue sauce in individual serving dishes. Dip rolls in sauce. These are great for lunch.

PORTUGUESE SWEET BREAD

2 packages active dry yeast
1 ²/₃ cups warm water
1 cup dry instant potato flakes
1 cup sugar
6 tablespoons melted margarine
  or butter
2 teaspoons salt

4 eggs
1 tablespoon finely shredded lemon or
  orange peel, or ¹/₂ tablespoon each
³/₄ cup raisins
³/₄ cup golden raisins
7 ¹/₂ cups all-purpose flour

In a large mixing bowl, soften yeast in warm water. Mix in potato flakes, sugar, melted margarine, salt, eggs, peel and raisins. Add flour until dough is no longer sticky, about 7¹/₂ cups. Knead with dough hook 2 to 3 minutes or by hand 10 minutes, until smooth. Put dough in a large, greased bowl, turning it once so it's greased on the top and bottom. Cover bowl with a towel.

Let dough rise 1¹/₂ hours or until double. Punch it down, and let it rise 10 minutes more. Divide dough into 3 large, round loaves or 4 smaller ones; place them on a greased cookie sheet with space between them. You can also braid the dough or form it into any shape.

Cover dough with a towel, and allow it to rise until almost double, about 45 minutes. Bake loaves in a preheated oven at 350° for 35 to 40 minutes, depending on number of loaves. Cover them with foil after the first 20 minutes so they won't get too brown.
Makes 3 or 4 loaves.

Note: This bread makes great toast. We enjoy giving these festive loaves to our neighbors for Christmas.

3 cups warm water
1 package dry yeast
3 tablespoons sugar

1 1/2 tablespoons salt
7 1/2 to 8 cups flour

In a large mixer bowl, dissolve yeast in 1 cup warm water. Add sugar and salt; let stand 5 minutes. Stir in 2 cups water and 3 cups flour, beating with the paddle on a heavy-duty mixer or by hand with a wooden spoon.

Add remaining flour a cup at a time. Knead with dough hook 4 to 6 minutes or 8 to 10 minutes by hand, until the dough feels smooth and elastic. Cover with a towel; let dough rise until almost tripled. Or make dough early in the morning, and let it rise all day. Shape dough into 4 baguettes (long, slender loaves). Let loaves rise about 45 minutes until doubled in size. Preheat oven to 450°. Bake for 15 minutes. Reduce temperature to 350°; bake for 30 more minutes or until golden brown. **Makes 4 loaves.**

Note: Freeze each baked loaf in foil. To reheat, loosen one end of foil and heat loaf at 375° until hot and crisp—about 20 minutes. You may also want to use this dough for **Pizza Roll-Ups** or **Veggie Pizza** instead of commercial frozen dough.

SWEDISH RYE BREAD

2 packages dry yeast
1/4 cup plus 1 teaspoon sugar
9 1/2 cups all-purpose flour
2 cups warm water
2 cups milk
5 tablespoons soft margarine
1/2 cup brown sugar

1/2 cup molasses
1 tablespoon salt
1 1/4 teaspoons anise seed
2 teaspoons caraway seed
3 cups rye flour
3 tablespoons dark corn syrup

Combine yeast, 1 teaspoon sugar, 1 1/2 cups all-purpose flour and 1 cup warm water in a small bowl. Cover, and let rise about 30 minutes.

In a small saucepan, scald 2 cups milk in remaining cup of warm water. Combine margarine, brown sugar, 1/4 cup white sugar, molasses, salt, anise seed, caraway seed, 1 cup all-purpose flour, rye flour and dark corn syrup in a large bowl. Stir scalded milk into this mixture. Let it cool until it's warm to the touch. Stir in yeast mixture.

Gradually stir in about 3 cups all-purpose flour until a ball forms. Then turn dough onto a hard surface and gradually mix in 4 more cups flour, kneading dough 8 to 10 minutes until it's smooth and elastic. Put dough into a greased bowl covered with a towel; let rise until double, about 50 minutes.

Divide dough to make 3 or 4 loaves. Put them in greased loaf pans, or shape dough into 5 or 6 small loaves and bake them on ungreased cookie sheets.

Let loaves rise about 45 minutes. Bake at 325° for about 40 to 50 minutes, depending on size and number of loaves. Rub a butter cube over tops of the warm loaves. Remove them from pans immediately and cool. **Makes 3 to 4 regular loaves or 5 to 6 small loaves**.

Note: These loaves are excellent as an alternative to cookies and fudge for Christmas gifts.

2 egg yolks
1 3/4 cups sugar
2 8-ounce packages cream cheese, softened
3 loaves Pepperidge Farm sandwich bread

(or other very firm, thin-sliced white bread)
1 pound (4 sticks) margarine
4 teaspoons ground cinnamon

Beat egg yolks and 1/2 cup sugar together; stir in cream cheese until smooth. Trim crusts from bread; use a rolling pin to flatten each slice.

Spread cheese mixture on a slice of bread; top with another slice to make a sandwich. Do the same with the remaining bread slices. Cut each sandwich lengthwise into 4 logs.

Melt margarine. Mix cinnamon and remaining 1 1/4 cups sugar in a bowl. Dip each log in melted margarine, and then in cinnamon sugar. Place on rimmed cookie sheets. Bake in a preheated 400° oven for 10 minutes. **Makes 80 to 100 logs.**

Note: Before baking logs, freeze them on rimmed cookie sheets; then put them in freezer bags. To serve, remove as many logs as you need from the bag. Put frozen logs on a cookie sheet or flat baking dish. Bake the same as above.

1 1/2 cups all-purpose flour
1/2 cup sugar
2 teaspoons baking powder
3/4 teaspoon salt
1 teaspoon ground cinnamon
1/2 teaspoon ground ginger
1/4 teaspoon ground cloves
1/2 cup raisins

1 egg
1/2 cup milk
1/2 cup canned pumpkin
1/4 cup salad oil

Topping
2 1/2 teaspoons sugar
1/2 teaspoon ground cinnamon

Stir flour, sugar, baking powder, salt and spices in a large mixing bowl until well combined. Then mix in raisins. Beat egg, milk, pumpkin and salad oil in a smaller bowl.

Pour pumpkin mixture into flour and spices, stirring only until combined. Fill lightly greased muffin cups 2/3 full. Mix sugar and cinnamon; sprinkle on muffins. Bake in a preheated 400° oven 20 to 25 minutes or until nicely browned. Serve warm. **Makes 12 muffins.**

AUNTIE TEETO'S WAFFLES

2 cups all-purpose flour (or substitute
 ½ cup whole wheat or buckwheat
 flour for ½ cup of the all-purpose
 flour)
1 teaspoon baking soda

1 teaspoon salt
2 eggs
1 ½ cups buttermilk
2 tablespoons vegetable oil

Preheat waffle iron, and spray with nonstick spray. Sift together flour, soda and salt. In a medium bowl, lightly beat eggs; stir in buttermilk and vegetable oil. Add liquid ingredients to flour mixture, stirring just to moisten. Pour a circle of batter about 5 inches in diameter into the center of a waffle iron. Bake according to waffle iron's instructions or until steaming stops, about 5 minutes. Serve with warmed maple syrup. **Makes 6 servings.**

Note: This recipe was given to Mimi by her ninety-four-year-old aunt, who used an equally old waffle iron. These waffles are great for Sunday supper for college students. Serve waffles with sausage and hot chocolate.

GOOD DAY GRANOLA

8 cups rolled oats (not instant)
1 ¼ cups firmly packed brown sugar
1 ½ cups unprocessed bran
1 ½ cups natural wheat germ (not
 toasted or honeyed)
¾ cup chopped walnuts

½ cup raw sunflower seeds
½ cup vegetable oil
¾ cup honey
2 teaspoons vanilla
2 cups raisins

Stir oats, brown sugar, bran, wheat germ, walnuts and sunflower seeds in a large bowl. Put vegetable oil, honey and vanilla in a small saucepan; heat, stirring till bubbly. Pour liquid over dry ingredients, mixing thoroughly.

Divide oat mixture evenly and spread on two rimmed cookie sheets. Bake in a pre-heated oven at 325° for 15 to 20 minutes, stirring once to keep granola evenly browned. While it cools, stir mixture several times to keep it from sticking together. When completely cool, add raisins. Store in an airtight container. **Makes about 16 cups.**

Note: This granola keeps for weeks and is yummy for breakfast or snacks.

BEVERAGES

ORANGE SPICED TEA

2 cups powdered orange drink mix
3/4 cup instant tea mix
1 teaspoon ground cinnamon

1 teaspoon ground cloves
1 2-quart package presweetened dry lemonade mix

   Mix all the above ingredients together. To serve, stir 2 heaping teaspoons of the mix into an 8-ounce mug of hot water or a 10-ounce glass of cold water. This drink is great hot or cold.

CRANBERRY TEA

1 cup cranberry juice
3 cups prepared iced tea

3 tablespoons lemon juice
1/4 cup sugar

   Combine all ingredients. Serve hot or cold. **Makes 1 quart.**

DESSERTS

BLUEBERRY PIE

1 10-ounce jar currant jelly
1 pint fresh blueberries
1 graham cracker crust, baked (see recipe below)

1 cup sour cream (or whipped topping for a sweeter pie)

Melt jelly in a saucepan over low heat. Add blueberries and stir. Pour into baked graham cracker crust. Spread sour cream on top, and refrigerate overnight. **Makes 6 to 8 servings.**

Note: This pie is so easy and so good!

GRAHAM CRACKER CRUST

1 1/2 cups crushed graham crackers
3 tablespoons sugar

1/3 cup melted margarine or butter

Crush graham crackers in a plastic bag, using a rolling pin. Mix crumbs with sugar and melted margarine. Press crumb mixture against bottom and sides of a 9-inch pie pan. Bake in a preheated oven at 350° for 10 minutes.

LOW-CALORIE CHOCOLATE CAKE

3 cups all-purpose flour
1/2 cup sugar
1/3 cup unsweetened cocoa powder
2 teaspoons baking soda
1 teaspoon salt
2 cups water

2 tablespoons white vinegar
4 teaspoons chocolate syrup
2 teaspoons vanilla
1/3 cup sugar
3/4 cup margarine
2 teaspoons vegetable oil

Preheat oven to 350°. Mix flour, sugar, cocoa, baking soda and salt; set aside. Mix water, vinegar, syrup and vanilla in a separate bowl; set aside. Cream sugar, margarine and vegetable oil in a large mixing bowl until fluffy. Alternate adding the dry and wet mixtures to the sugar and vegetable oil, beating well. Spray a Bundt pan with nonstick spray. Pour batter into Bundt pan, and bake 40 minutes. Serve with whipped cream or whipped topping if desired.

1/2 cup margarine
1/2 cup vegetable oil
1/4 cup unsweetened cocoa powder
1 cup water
1 teaspoon baking soda
1/2 cup buttermilk

1 teaspoon ground cinnamon
2 cups all-purpose flour
2 cups sugar
2 eggs
1 teaspoon vanilla
1/2 teaspoon salt

SPRING CAKE

Preheat oven to 400°. Bring margarine, vegetable oil, cocoa powder and water to a boil in a large saucepan, stirring constantly. Remove pan from stove. Stir baking soda into buttermilk, adding to cocoa mixture along with cinnamon, flour, sugar, eggs, vanilla and salt. Stir until well mixed. Pour batter into a greased and floured 13x9x2-inch baking pan. Bake for 20 to 25 minutes. Ice with **Cocoa Frosting** while cake is still warm. **Makes 12 servings.**

1/2 cup margarine
1/3 cup buttermilk
1/4 cup unsweetened cocoa powder

1 16-ounce box powdered sugar
1 teaspoon vanilla
Nuts (optional)

COCOA FROSTING

Bring margarine, buttermilk and cocoa to boil in a medium saucepan. Remove pan from heat. Beat in powdered sugar and vanilla; while still warm pour on cake. Top with nuts, if desired.

Note: Bake this cake on the day a family member sees the first sign of spring. This cake and frosting freeze well.

JIFFY SALAD

1 small head lettuce
2 to 3 hard-cooked eggs

Dressing
¼ teaspoon salt
¼ teaspoon pepper

¼ cup salad oil
2 tablespoons vinegar
1 teaspoon soy sauce
1 tablespoon chopped fresh parsley
¼ cup grated Parmesan cheese

Wash and shred lettuce; put in a salad bowl. Chop hard-cooked eggs; add to lettuce. Mix remaining ingredients for dressing. Toss lettuce, eggs and dressing. **Serves 4.**

CRANBERRY CREAM SALAD

1 cup heavy whipping cream, chilled
3 tablespoons sugar
2 3-ounce packages cream cheese

1 16-ounce can whole cranberry sauce
1 8-ounce can crushed pineapple, drained

Whip cream and sugar in a chilled bowl until stiff peaks form. Mix in remaining ingredients. Pour into a loaf pan and freeze. To serve, thaw slightly and cut into slices. Serve as a dessert or salad on lettuce leaves. **Makes 8 to 10 servings.**

CINNAMON APPLESAUCE SALAD

2 3-ounce packages lemon gelatin
½ cup red hots (cinnamon or candy imperials)

2 cups unsweetened applesauce
1 tablespoon lemon juice
Dash of salt

Dissolve gelatin and red hots in 3 cups boiling water, stirring until they dissolve. Stir in applesauce, lemon juice and salt. Chill until set in a square 8x8x1 ½-inch pan or gelatin mold. **Makes 9 servings**.

1 17-ounce can apricots

1 20-ounce can unsweetened crushed pineapple

1 cup juice or syrup drained from apricots and pineapple

1/2 cup sugar

1 16-ounce package unsweetened, whole frozen strawberries

3 bananas, sliced

1 6-ounce can frozen orange juice concentrate

2 tablespoons lemon juice

Drain apricots and pineapple, reserving 1 cup of combined syrup. Cook syrup and sugar over medium heat about 5 minutes, stirring until sugar dissolves. Partially thaw strawberries until they can be separated. Add about 2 cups apricots, pineapple, strawberries, sliced bananas, syrup, sugar, orange juice concentrate and lemon juice to the blender at a time. Cover and puree until smooth and slightly chunky; then pour each batch of fruit mixture into a large bowl. When all fruit has been blended, stir together. Line 30 muffin cups with paper baking cups. Ladle fruit mixture into paper cups. Freeze until solid.

When frozen, turn over muffin tins, and punch out frozen fruit cups with your thumb. Package frozen fruit cups in freezer bags. Remove cups from freezer 20 minutes before serving as a salad or dessert. **Makes 30.**

Note: Put ice cream sticks in each cup before freezing to make sherbet treats.

1 16-ounce can sliced peaches with syrup

1 16-ounce can pear halves with syrup

1 15-ounce can pineapple chunks with syrup

1/2 cup orange marmalade

1 3-inch cinnamon stick

1/2 teaspoon ground nutmeg

1/4 teaspoon ground cloves

HOT SPICED FRUIT

Mix all the above ingredients with liquid in a large saucepan. Bring to a boil; reduce heat. Cover and simmer 1 hour. Try fixing this in a crockpot. Imagine the aroma! **Makes 12 servings.**

Note: Eat this warm as a fruit sauce, or it's good served over sliced ham or ice cream.

SMOKY CORN CHOWDER

½ cup chopped yellow onion
4 tablespoons butter or margarine
¼ cup all-purpose flour
1 ¼ teaspoons salt
¼ teaspoon pepper
4 cups milk

1 17-ounce can whole-kernel corn, drained
4 smoked sausage links, sliced (6-ounce package)
1 8-ounce can lima beans (optional)

In a saucepan, sauté onion in butter until tender but not brown. Stir in flour, salt and pepper. Add milk all at once. Bring to a boil, stirring constantly until thick and bubbly, about 1 minute. Stir in corn, sausage and lima beans. Reduce heat; simmer 10 minutes. **Makes 6 servings.**

Note: Spread a picnic blanket on the floor, and have a family picnic in front of the fireplace on a winter night. Serve **Smoky Corn Chowder** with fresh-baked bread. Toast marshmallows for dessert.

SALSA DE LENTEJAS

⅔ cup chopped onion
1 scant teaspoon (1 small clove) minced garlic
1 tablespoon vegetable oil
¾ cup dried lentils, washed
2 cups water
2 beef bouillon cubes
⅛ teaspoon ground cayenne pepper

⅛ teaspoon freshly ground black pepper
½ teaspoon dried basil leaves, crumbled
½ teaspoon dried oregano leaves, crumbled
2 teaspoons white vinegar
1 8-ounce can tomato sauce
1 6-ounce can tomato paste

In a large saucepan, sauté onion and garlic in vegetable oil for about 5 minutes. Add lentils, water, beef bouillon cubes, cayenne and black pepper. Cover and simmer for 30 minutes. Add basil, oregano, vinegar, tomato sauce and tomato paste, and simmer uncovered about 1 hour, stirring occasionally. **Makes 5 servings**.

Note: This is a tasty but hot dish!

VEGETABLES

6 baking potatoes
Salt and pepper
Margarine or butter
Milk
¼ cup chopped onion

¾ cup grated cheddar cheese
¾ cup grated Monterey Jack cheese
1 box frozen, chopped spinach, thawed
   and pressed dry

Prepare and bake 6 baking potatoes in a preheated 400° oven for 1 hour. While potatoes are still hot, slice each potato in half lengthwise. Carefully scoop pulp into a large mixing bowl, leaving a thin shell. Mash potatoes, adding salt, pepper and margarine to taste and milk as needed. Stir in onion, cheddar and Jack cheeses and spinach. Spoon potato mixture back into the shells.

Bake potato halves in a preheated 400° oven for 20 minutes or until lightly browned. Serve immediately. Or freeze potatoes before reheating them. To serve potatoes, remove as many as needed. Allow to thaw, place on a rimmed cookie sheet or in a baking dish. Bake in a preheated 400° oven about 20 minutes or until lightly browned. **Makes 12 servings.**

1 to 1 ½ pounds fresh asparagus
Salt and pepper (lemon pepper, if
   desired)

3 tablespoons butter

Rinse asparagus, and trim off rough ends. Place spears in one or two layers in a baking pan. Sprinkle with salt and pepper, and dot with butter. Cover with foil, and bake 30 minutes in a preheated oven at 300°. The asparagus will be crunchy and not lose color. **Makes 6 to 8 servings.**

MARINATED VEGGIES

1 large stalk fresh broccoli
1 3 1/2-ounce can medium, pitted ripe olives, drained
1 16-ounce can green beans, drained
1 16-ounce can julienned carrots, drained
6 halved, cherry tomatoes
1/4 pound sliced, fresh mushrooms

Marinade
1 cup cider vinegar
1 cup salad oil
1 minced, large garlic clove
3/4 teaspoon dried basil leaves
3/4 teaspoon dried oregano leaves
3/4 teaspoon salt
1/4 teaspoon pepper
1/2 minced, small onion

Chop broccoli florets and a small portion of the upper stalk. Cook broccoli 5 minutes or until slightly crisp. Combine broccoli and remaining vegetables in a 2-quart casserole dish.

Mix marinade in a small saucepan, bring to a boil, reduce heat, and simmer for 10 minutes. Pour marinade over vegetables, toss, and refrigerate for several hours until chilled.

Note: Add your favorite cooked, small pasta for a **Presto Pasta Salad.**

CHAPTER 7

"The eyes of all look to you, and you give them their food at the proper time. You open your hand and satisfy the desires of every living thing"

(Psalm 145:15-16, NIV).

CHOOSING RECIPES

Once you've tried *Once-a-Month Cooking*, you may want to adapt it to your recipes. The following suggestions will help you set up your system.

Choose dishes that freeze well. (See the section on freezer storage tips in chapter 8.) Take into consideration that it's not safe to thaw meat, work with it, leave it raw, and then refreeze it. You must cook meat before freezing it again. But if you buy fresh meat, you can add ingredients and freeze the meat raw.

Start with your family's favorite recipes rather than exotic, new dishes. Or test recipes before you create your own plan. Be sure to pick simple recipes rather than ones that require many complicated steps. You need to keep your assembly order and food preparation as easy as possible. Otherwise, you'll be spending too much time in the kitchen and defeating your purpose of saving time.

Make sure you have a nice variety of recipes. You don't want to serve similar entrées too close together, such as two stews or three creamy noodle casseroles. If you don't mind having the same dish twice in a month, double the recipe for a favorite entrée, divide it in half, and freeze it. You may also want to consider dishes that could be used for both lunch and dinner or could be taken to work or reheated in a microwave oven.

If you enjoy the ministry of hospitality, choose dishes that work well for larger groups or could be taken to someone who is sick or has a special need.

After you decide what recipes you want to try, divide them into groups such as chicken, beef, fish, pork, meatless or miscellaneous. This will show you how many recipes you have in each category. You may have too many chicken dishes or casseroles and need to balance your recipes by adding other kinds of meats or different types of dishes. You may also want to set up your system for only a week's worth of dishes rather than two weeks or a month.

One mother who uses the method finds that it works well to prepare all the dishes in a category at the same time—all the beef recipes in one afternoon, for example, and all the recipes in another category the next day.

Finally, make sure the ingredients called for in the recipes fit your budget. Some meats, especially fish, can be expensive.

First, reproduce and use the blank calendar we've included in this chapter. When you record the recipes on it, write them in pencil, because you may need to change them around.

Second, check your schedule for days you know you'll be away from home and won't need to prepare meals; then cross off those dates. Take into account the nights you'll need to prepare something quick because you or your kids have meetings or activities. Pencil in easy-to-prepare dishes for those times. Make note of holidays or special occasions, such as a birthday or anniversary, you'll need to plan for.

Third, organize your recipes by category, such as beef, chicken or miscellaneous, before filling out the menu calendar. Make sure you have a variety of meats and kinds of dishes for each week.

If you plan to have company, select the recipes you would use for the occasion.

Write those entrées on the appropriate dates. Do the same with dishes you would like to take to a friend or use for a potluck. If Mom and Dad plan to be out but the kids will be eating at home, write in dishes they particularly like and can finish preparing easily.

If some dishes suit a particular day of the week, such as quiche on Sunday, add those recipes to the appropriate days. Then fill out the calendar with your recipes.

Finally, you may want to create your own plan without considering your schedule or special occasions. You would just like to prepare two weeks or a month of meals at once and have them in your freezer. If you do that, you may still want to fill out a calendar so you have a variety of meals scheduled and as a way to keep track of the ones you've made. Check them off as you serve them to your family.

MAKING A MENU CALENDAR

Now use your recipes to compile your shopping and staples lists. You'll need a sheet of paper for each list. It may help to categorize your grocery list with the same headings we've used: Canned Goods; Grains, Pasta and Rice; Dry Ingredients and Seasonings; Dairy Products; Meat and Poultry; and Produce. Alphabetizing the items under each catagory in your shopping list makes it easier to follow.

You can also categorize your list by

aisles or areas in your favorite supermarket. If you don't want to recopy your list, you can categorize by highlighting items with different colored marking pens: pink for produce, brown for meat, green for canned goods and yellow for bakery.

To figure what food you'll need, check ingredients in each recipe, and record all the items on either the grocery shopping or staples lists. For example, if a recipe calls for cinnamon and you already have

FIGURING SHOPPING AND STAPLES LISTS

it, put it on the staples list. But add it to the shopping list if you don't have it. If 2 1/2 pounds of chicken pieces are required, put them on the shopping list. For items needed for more than one recipe, such as onions, chicken pieces or tomato sauce, keep a running tally of quantities needed, and then figure the total. (See Equivalent Measures in chapter 8 for how to convert size of portions.)

Finally, be sure to list freezer bags or containers for each entrée. Then add the ones you'll need to your shopping list.

SETTING UP AN ASSEMBLY ORDER

Once you've filled in your calendar, check instructions in **The Day Before Cooking Day** and **Cooking Day Assembly Order** for the two-week and one-month plans to help you make out your own assembly order.

Write or type your recipes on large, blank index cards. Then spread the recipes on a table and arrange them in an order that will flow well when you're doing the preparation work. Group recipes that use similar ingredients, particularly meats.

Once you have your recipes in order, go through each one, tallying the total amount of each food item you'll need to process: how many cups of cheddar cheese to grate, carrots to shred or ground beef to brown.

When you write out the assembly order, try to work with two or three recipes in the same category at a time, such as all the ground beef recipes or all the chicken. Record all the ingredients you'll need to store or freeze until the accompanying dishes are served. List any tasks you'll need to do the day before cooking day, such as cooking all the chicken or soaking the pinto beans. You may also want to plan to do most of the chopping, grating, shredding and slicing tasks the day before.

Then make out an assembly order with directions for how to proceed from one recipe to the next. If you haven't scheduled the chopping and slicing tasks for the day before, plan to do them the first thing on cooking day. Recipes that require longer cooking, such as soups or stews, should also be started right away.

Make sure you'll have enough stove burners to cook dishes in a particular group at the same time. Whenever possible, combine steps for several dishes: Cook rice for two dishes; sauté all onions at once.

Continue through all the recipes until you have completed your assembly order. Allow for time between groups of recipes so you can take some breaks.

The first time you try your own plan, take a few extra minutes to write out any corrections in the recipes or procedures. Then the next time you cook, it will go even smoother.

The following suggestions will help you revise your plan:

1. Correct the order of tasks if they weren't easy to follow or in the right order. If you would do any part of the procedure differently, state what you would do.

2. If you should have prepared some dishes sooner or later in the process, make note of it.

3. Rework your plan if you had too many or too few dishes to prepare at once.

4. Write out new directions if they were difficult to follow in any of the sections.

5. If needed, correct ingredient amounts.

EVALUATING YOUR PLAN

A computer is an excellent way to store your own recipes and the ones in this book. Planning a month's cycle of meals and making out a calendar will also be easier on a computer.

One good software program we've found is Micro Kitchen Companion, distributed by Lifestyle Software, 63 Orange St., St. Augustine, Florida 32084. The toll-free number is 1-800-289-1157. It's a data base program with a recipe disk and is available for the IBM, Commodore, Apple, Macintosh and Atari computers.

It can be used to produce a shopping list by grocery store aisles, reduce or increase the size of portions, and sort recipes by main ingredients and several other categories.

Many services and products are being developed that can be of great help to the once-a-month cook. You might investigate telephone, fax or computer ordering from your supermarket. These systems are not mistake proof, but shopping this way and having groceries delivered can be a real advantage.

USING THE COMPUTER

MENU CALENDAR

SUN.	MON.	TUES.	WED.	THURS.	FRI.	SAT.

CHAPTER 8

"And if you spend yourselves in behalf of
the hungry and satisfy the needs of the
oppressed, then your light will rise in the
darkness, and your night will become like
the noonday"

(Isaiah 58:10, NIV).

EQUIVALENT MEASURES

1 tablespoon = 3 teaspoons, 1/2 fluid ounce

2 tablespoons = 1 fluid ounce

4 tablespoons = 1/4 cup

5 1/3 tablespoons = 1/3 cup

8 tablespoons = 1/2 cup

12 tablespoons = 3/4 cup

16 tablespoons = 1 cup

1 cup = 1/2 pint, 8 fluid ounces

2 cups = 1 pint

4 cups = 1 quart

4 quarts = 1 liquid gallon

1 pound lean ground beef or sausage browned = 2 1/2 cups

1 pound ground ham = 2 1/2 cups

1 pound cubed ham = 3 cups

1 cooked, deboned whole chicken (about 4 pounds) = 4 1/2 cups

1 cooked, deboned whole chicken (about 5 pounds) = 6 cups

1 medium yellow onion, chopped = 1 1/4 cups

1 medium yellow onion, chopped and sautéed = 3/4 cup

1 medium green pepper, chopped = 1 cup

1 pound cheese, grated = 4 cups

3 ounces fresh mushrooms, sliced = 1 cup

1 pound zucchini, diced = 1 1/2 cups

1 medium clove garlic, minced = 1 teaspoon

Frozen foods keep their natural color, flavor and nutritive qualities better than canned or dried foods. Freezing also stops the bacterial action in fresh food that causes it to spoil.

Food kept in the freezer too long may not taste right, but it shouldn't make you sick. However, it's not safe to thaw food, especially meat, and then refreeze it without first cooking it.

Frozen food that has been stored in moisture-proof containers with airtight lids or seals will keep its color and flavor much longer. You'll get the best results with products made for freezer use: plastic containers with lids; heavy aluminum foil; heavy plastic bags; freezer wraps and tape. Glass jars with lids (leave head space) also work well.

Avoid using regular waxed paper; lightweight aluminum foil; regular plastic wrap or cellophane; cartons from cottage cheese, ice cream or milk; ordinary butcher paper; the plastic film used on packaged meats; plastic produce bags from the supermarket.

Follow these helpful hints for freezing foods:

Freeze food quickly to 0° or below.

Post a dated list of food on the freezer door, and keep it current.

Use frozen food within a month to six weeks. Some seasonings become stronger while frozen, and some weaker. The degree of change is minimized if food is not left frozen too long.

Thaw, heat and serve food in rapid succession.

Allow hot foods to cool to room temperature before freezing.

Blanch or precook all vegetables before freezing to stop enzyme action and to keep them from becoming discolored and mushy. Drain blanched vegetables before freezing them.

Thaw foods in the refrigerator or microwave whenever possible. Thawing in the refrigerator will take twice as long as on the counter, but it's much safer. Thawing time will vary according to the thickness or quantity of food in the container.

Don't freeze the following foods. They will change color, texture or separate in some way during the freezing or thawing process:

Raw salad vegetables (such as lettuce, radishes, tomatoes).

Raw eggs in their shells or hard-cooked eggs.

Raw potatoes or boiled white potatoes (they turn black).

Commercial cottage cheese.

Gelatin salads or desserts.

Icing made with egg whites, boiled frostings or cakes with cream fillings.

Instant rice (it dissolves and becomes too mushy.) You can freeze regular cooked rice.

Custard pies, cream pies or pies with meringue.

MORE FREEZER STORAGE TIPS

VIDEOS

A thirty-minute videotape of Mimi Wilson demonstrating the once-a-month cooking method is available for purchase or for a two-week rental. The video is helpful for those who need motivation to do once-a-month cooking, feel apprehensive about trying it or to use as a program for womens' groups.

A forty-five-minute videotape of Mimi Wilson speaking on "The Ministry of Hospitality" is also available. This tape is accompanied by a five-week study guide for use in Bible study groups. The video covers making use of available resources for hospitality, maintaining a welcoming attitude, involving children, understanding the differences between hospitality and entertainment, and discovering the rewards of being hospitable.

Please send videotape inquiries to Mardell Peterson, 305 W. Caley Circle, Littleton, Colorado 80120; or phone (303) 794-2744.

INDEX